GARDENERS' WORLD

MAKING THE MOST OF
CLIMBING PLANTS

GARDENERS' WORLD

MAKING THE MOST OF
CLIMBING PLANTS

Practical Projects for Arches, Arbours,
Pergolas and Trellis

SUE FISHER

BBC BOOKS

BBC Books would like to thank the following for providing photographs and for permission to reproduce copyright material. While every effort has been made to trace and acknowledge all copyright holders, we would like to apologise should there have been any errors or omissions

Lynne Brotchie/The Garden Picture Library 79; Linda Burgess/The Garden Picture Library 55; Eric Crichton 22–23; John Glover 10, 34, 35, 66L, 87, 102, 103, 107, 111, 115; Jerry Harpur 6–7 (Designer: Christopher & Asson), 11, 15, 18–19, 27, 46–47, 90, 99, 106, 114, 118, 122; Lamontagne/The Garden Picture Library 66R–67; Jane Legate/The Garden Picture Library 58; Zara McCalmont/The Garden Picture Library 39; Clive Nichols 59, 74, 94, 95, 98; J.S. Sira/The Garden Picture Library 2, 50–51; Ron Sutherland/The Garden Picture Library 62–63, 70–71; Steven Wooster/The Garden Picture Library 30–31, 42–43, 83.

Published by BBC Books,
an imprint of BBC Worldwide Publishing.
BBC Worldwide Limited, Woodlands,
80 Wood Lane, London W12 0TT

ISBN 0 563 37189 7

Designed by BBC Books and Keith Watson
Illustrations by Jane Craddock-Watson

Set in Bembo 11 on 15pt

Printed and bound in Great Britain by Butler & Tanner Limited, Frome
Colour separations by Radstock Reproductions Ltd, Midsomer Norton
Cover printed by Clays ltd, St Ives plc

Contents

Introduction

~

Just about every garden has enormous untapped potential for growing on the vertical. Whatever the size of your plot, there is bound to be a place for some sort of upright feature, be it a handsome arch to enhance a path, a pergola over a patio, an arbour of scented plants or just a few pots of climbers for an unusual patio display. Whether you're starting from scratch or you just want to give your garden a facelift with a new feature or some climbing plants, there is something here for everyone. Apart from giving your garden a whole new look, where space is limited – as it so often is in today's gardens – climbing plants make it possible for the sky really to be the limit.

The practical projects that form the backbone of this book offer a wide selection of attractive structures for you to choose from and construct. Ten different themes are covered in detail in a range of styles from rustic to modern, and each one is designed in project form to make the process as straightforward as possible from beginning to end. There is a shopping list of materials and equipment, followed by step-by-step instructions

~

A little wooden arbour, complete with roof and garlanded with a climbing rose, makes a wonderfully secluded retreat.

accompanied by illustrations to lead you through the entire construction process. Finally, to take the headaches out of choosing the right plants to grace your new structure, there is a selection of the best plants for each one. There is extra practical information too, on how to plant and care for your climbers and how to look after your structure in future years.

As well as the detailed planting information that accompanies each project, there is an easy-reference directory of the best climbers and wall plants for the garden. There is absolutely nothing to beat these plants for sheer versatility. The range is huge, with a wealth of foliage variations and flower colours that can be blended to create a pageant of colour for every month. Combine these glorious plants with a handsome structure and you'll have a feature that will transform your garden right through the year.

Planning and designing the vertical garden

Whether you are creating the bones of a new garden or looking to give your existing one a boost with a fresh feature or two, there are many different ways in which to incorporate climbing plants and vertical structures into the garden.

The obvious place to start is with the ready-made sites that are simply begging to be clothed with plants, such as existing walls and fences. Where these sites are paved at the base, it may be possible to lift a slab or two to create a small area in which to plant. Failing that,

use large containers like wooden half-barrels that are ideal for permanent plants. Low walls and fences can easily be extended upwards by the addition of a piece of trellis to the top.

Then look round the garden to assess suitable sites for a large structure such as a pergola, arch or arbour, starting with the area surrounding the house itself. A south-facing patio can often be too sun-baked for comfort in summer, and the beams of a plant-clad pergola can cast a pleasant, dappled shade (see page 31). Alternatively, if you have a shady, north-facing patio, it is good to have some-where to sit in a sunnier part of the garden, such as the beamed arbour featured on page 38. A long pathway running alongside or away from the house can be turned into a real feature with a long pergola like the one shown on page 22.

Generally all but the tiniest gardens really benefit from being divided into different sections, so that in effect you can walk from one 'room' into the next. Arches are perfect for creating a plant-clad doorway between the different sections and accentuating the feeling of transition from one to another.

The theme of dividers can be taken one step further by the use of trellis screens. Use them either in a purely ornamental context, such as the one pictured on page 42, or on a more practical level to screen off any unsightly objects such as a shed, oil tank, dustbins and/or compost heaps.

Smaller features can be incorporated in many places around the garden. Such features include freestanding supports like tripods and obelisks, which can be dropped into a border and clothed with quick-growing climbers to provide instant height. This is particularly valuable in a new garden where shrubs and other plants take several years to reach the same height. A similar effect can be achieved in containers where climbers can be used to make a handsome patio display.

Their economic use of ground space make climbers excellent for small spaces, and they can double up with existing plants to inject even more colour and interest into the garden. Established shrubs, conifers and trees can all support climbers for an extra splash of flowers, and even low-growing plants such as winter-flowering heathers or ground-covering cotoneasters can be draped with a herbaceous climber to cheer them up during the summer months.

Once you've decided where to site your new features, the next step is to consider the type of structure you want to construct and whether it is to be utilitarian or decorative in appearance. To a certain extent this will depend on the amount of time and money you wish to spend and the level of your DIY skills. For example, the type of brick-pillared pergola on page 31 obviously takes more time, money and skill to construct than the wooden pergola on page 22. It depends too on whether the structure is intended primar-ily as a support for the plants, in which case there is not a great deal of point in taking a lot of time and trouble to make an intricate, finely decorated frame-work that will soon disappear under a smothering of foliage! If the structure itself is to take centre stage, it's a good idea to plant

sparingly to enhance rather than conceal it.

If you're not at all keen on constructing a major feature yourself, don't despair if you've never picked up a saw or hammer before. A number of manufacturers produce pergolas, arches, arbours and other features in kit form, all ready to be put together, and often priced very competitively.

Success with plants

Climbers and wall shrubs are exceptionally versatile plants that offer a huge variety of flower and foliage colour. Outlined below are a few useful pointers to help you get the most from your plants.

Checking the aspect: sun or shade

Identifying the aspect – the direction in which a site faces – is important as a number of plants are very particular about the amount of sun they require. There are plants to suit every spot in the garden, but the right plant needs to be matched to the right place. Although a few go-anywhere plants like ivy and pyracantha are happy in sun or shade, others such as passion flower and wisteria need plenty of sun in order to produce a splendid show of flowers, while a few such as *Tropaeolum speciosum* will shrivel and sulk in a sunny spot. It's well worth spending money on good plants, but make sure you don't waste your cash by putting a plant where it will register its disapproval by dying! Each plant listing in the directory includes details of any special cultural preferences.

Choose flower and foliage colours to complement their background. Wisteria, with its long blue racemes of flower, looks magnificent against a buff-coloured wall.

Plant habit

There are three main ways in which plants climb, and it's useful to identify the habit of a particular plant in order to match it to the right framework. There are those plants that are self-clinging by means of aerial roots or adhesive pads, such as ivy and Virginia creeper, and they rarely need any support; all you need to do is point the young plant in the right direction by using short canes. Twining plants such as jasmine and runner beans have stems which wind upwards, so they need vertical wires or trellis. Lastly, plants with tendrils or curling leaf stems, such as clematis, need closely spaced wires, trellis or mesh up which to climb.

Two other plant groups also need to be considered. They are those plants such as roses which 'climb' by means of long stems, usually assisted by their prickles that hook on to the support, though they do benefit from regular tying in. Lastly there are wall shrubs that need to be tied on to a support such as wires or trellis, sometimes coupled with a little pruning to keep their growth flat rather than bushy.

Actinidia kolomikta, with its unusual variegated leaves, contrasts beautifully with golden foliage.

Designing with colour

In order to achieve the best effects from your plants, it's worth looking at the flower and foliage colours in relation to where the plants will be growing in the garden. This is particularly true if you intend growing climbers against a strongly coloured background such as a wall or fence. Red-brick walls and dark-stained fences make an excellent backdrop for pale or variegated foliage and flowers. Buff-coloured walls and fences are perfect for darker foliage and blue, purple or violet flowers. White or grey walls look superb with warmer colours such as red and pink. Bare, leafless winter stems show up most against a pale background, so it's often better to opt for a fair proportion of evergreens in more prominent sites.

Planning a colour scheme in advance can pay dividends, particularly in a small garden. Putting bright colours near the house and pale ones further away gives the illusion of the space being larger than it actually is. It's also a good idea to limit the number of colours in a small area, rather than cramming in lots of different ones and creating a muddled overall impression.

Screening with climbers

On a purely practical level, climbers are excellent for creating a screen to give privacy. Whereas even the quickest-growing hedge takes a good few years to begin to make an impact, fast-growing climbers supported on a framework can make a substantial difference in providing a worthwhile screen even in their first year.

Another important consideration is that, where space is limited, such a screen will take up far less room widthways than a bulky hedge. If there is just a small area to be screened − a single overlooking window, for example − a plant-clad tripod of rustic poles or a wrought-iron obelisk often does the job admirably.

Within the garden, screening unsightly objects is frequently a prime objective. Virtually every garden has some clutter of everyday living − rubbish bins, tools, a shed or an oil tank − which can soon be hidden by a couple of pieces of trellis clothed with climbers.

Vigorous climbers that are ideal for screening include clematis species such as *C. montana* and *C. orientalis*, roses such as 'Paul's Himalayan Musk' and, so long as you have plenty of room, the incredibly rampant Russian vine (*Polygonum baldschuanicum*) which certainly earns its common name of mile-a-minute. Ivies take a year or so to start growing at any speed, but they're well worth including in order to have some long-lasting, handsome, evergreen foliage.

Practical matters

Preparing the ground

All plants benefit from thorough soil preparation before planting to get them off to a flying start in life. Such advance preparation is particularly important with climbers, however, as they have a limited area of ground from which to extract all the water and nutrients that they need in order to sustain a comparatively large amount of growth. Special attention should be given to the borders that are adjacent to walls and fences, as they are usually limited in size and often have poorer-quality soil than elsewhere in the garden. The problem is compounded by the fact that a house wall with overhanging eaves keeps off a considerable amount of rain that falls.

To prepare the ground for planting, dig the soil to two spades' depth (or two spits deep), shovelling the top layer to one side. This keeps the good-quality, humus-rich topsoil separate from any poorer-quality subsoil. Pull out any weeds, being particularly careful to remove every bit of the roots of perennial weeds such as bindweed or ground elder because even a centimetre of root will produce a new plant. Fork over the second layer of soil, break up any compacted lumps and take out any brickbats, stones or large lumps of debris. Then dig in plenty of organic matter such as well-rotted manure, garden compost or a proprietary planting compost. A generous addition of organic matter works wonders on any type of soil: on light, free-draining soils it holds water and nutrients that would otherwise drain out quickly, and on heavy clay or silty ground it helps open out and improve the soil structure. Finish by shovelling back the top spit of soil and levelling it roughly with a rake.

Planting and aftercare

To get the plant off to a good start, give its rootball a good soaking by standing it in a bucket of water for an hour or two before planting. Dig a hole slightly larger than the rootball and mix some slow-release fertilizer into the bottom of the hole and into the excavated soil. If planting against a wall, dig the hole about 30 cm (12 in) away from it as the bricks will take vital moisture away from the plant's roots. Gently knock the plant out of its pot, which I find is best done by spreading one hand across the surface of the pot, upending the plant and tapping the edge of the pot on a wall or post. If there is a mass of roots spiralling around the bottom of the rootball, spread them out first, then put the plant in the prepared hole so that the top of the rootball is level with the ground. Clematis are the main exception to this rule as they benefit from being planted 5–10 cm (2–4 in) deeper. Backfill the planting hole, firming the soil to avoid leaving any air pockets, and give the plant a thorough watering. Mulching the ground with a 5 cm (2 in) layer of chipped bark or compost will help the plant establish as the mulch slows water loss by evaporation and discourages weeds.

Container-grown plants can be planted at any time of the year, while bare-rooted ones that are usually sold by mail order can be supplied only in autumn and winter while they are dormant. Regardless of whether they are container-grown or bare-rooted, autumn is the optimum time to put in hardy plants as the soil is then warm and moist, enabling them to make plenty of root growth and become well established in time for an explosion of growth the next spring. The exceptions are plants that are subject to frost damage if the weather is severe, such as *Ceanothus, Solanum jasminoïdes* and *Trachelospermum,* and they are best planted in spring so that they have a full season to establish before the winter frosts begin.

The amount of aftercare depends on the planting time. Plants put in through spring and summer will need frequent watering, even daily during hot weather, while those planted in autumn will need watering in the following spring only if it is dry. Watering can be made more straightforward by using a large, plastic, mineral-water bottle to be sure that the water goes directly to the roots. Simply remove the top, cut the base off the bottle and sink it upside-down in the ground next to the rootball, then just fill it right up at each watering. If you have lots of new plants, however, consider setting up an irrigation system. There are some excellent kits now available for the ordinary garden, and once you have set it all up, all you'll need to do is to turn on the tap. Even better, for when you're away from home, you can add a timing device that will do the job for you!

Planting climbers to grow through established plants

Large, well-grown plants like trees, shrubs and conifers all make excellent hosts for climbers. The problem is that the surrounding soil tends to be thoroughly colonized with roots, so any new plant is going to have a tough time competing with them for water and nutrients.

To make life easier for a new climber, it is best sited at the edge of the larger plant's canopy of branches, rather than near its trunk where the roots are usually at their most dense. From here the climber can be trained up into the branches by means of canes, string or wires. Unless the climber is a real sun-lover, plant it on the north side of its host if possible where the soil will be cooler and damper. Prepare the ground by digging out an area at least 60 cm (24 in) square and filling with fresh topsoil mixed with lots of organic matter. For an even better chance of success, frame the planting pit with a bottomless wooden box sunk into the ground. By the time the wood rots, the climber should be well established and able to hold its own in competition with other plants.

Annual maintenance of plants

Climbers and wall plants need only a little attention each year to keep them in good health. In early spring mulch the soil with a 5-cm (2-in) layer of organic matter such as compost, manure or chipped bark, which will keep the soil in good condition, reduce water loss and discourage weeds. At the same time, put on some slow-release fertilizer and rake or hoe it into the soil. During long periods of dry weather established plants will benefit from a thorough watering once or twice a week. Even in winter don't overlook the need for occasional watering if rain is short.

~

Grow climbers through other plants for extra colour. A blue-grey conifer makes an ideal companion for Clematis viticella *'Abundance', while on the left* C. v. *'Etoile Violette' scrambles over a* Senecio.

Pruning and training

Immediately after planting, the stems of the climber or wall plant should be spread out and tied on to its support. During the growing season train or tie in the new shoots regularly while they are still young and supple, as they will soon grow together to form a congested mass. With self-clinging climbers such as ivy and Virginia creeper, the stems are best trained on to the wall by means of canes in order to give them a secure base from which to scramble up.

Many climbers and wall shrubs benefit from annual pruning to encourage flowers and new healthy growth, and to control and restrict existing growth. Details on the pruning of individual plants are given along with each plant's description in the Plant Directory on page 85. For all plants, remove dead, diseased or damaged wood, and take out any stems that cross as they can rub against each other, opening wounds that can become diseased.

Secateurs are usually adequate for most pruning jobs, though thick branches are best dealt with using long-handled loppers or a pruning saw. If you need to tackle a large, well-established climber from a ladder, do make sure that its feet are securely placed and preferably braced against a firm object such as a metal post hammered into the ground. Ideally enlist a helper to hold the ladder for you. To protect your eyes from whippy, thorny stems, it's a good idea to wear plastic safety goggles, and if you are tackling a large, overgrown plant full of dead foliage, it's worth wearing a face mask to avoid breathing in the dust. You may feel a bit daft in all this protective clothing, but it's much better than suffering an injury.

Types of wooden fencing

Wooden fencing makes an excellent boundary to a garden and it can also be used to break it into sections or to create privacy. It can look rather stark when it is first put up, though its straight lines can soon be softened with a wealth of climbing plants.

There are a number of different styles available. Closeboard fencing is ideal for complete privacy. The most popular type is the horizontal overlap design, often called larch lap, and this tends to be most economical. However it is worth checking that the overlapping boards are reasonably sound or it could begin to deteriorate within a few years. Vertical boarding is much more stout but is also correspondingly more expensive.

Bamboo and wattle screens look very attractive and they are also good for creating privacy. Although they can be combined with climbers, they tend to look best when used as a background to border plants.

Rustic fencing is usually made of poles sawn in half lengthways. Designs usually come in a range of decorative styles, or you could just make your own post and rail fencing. The more open the design is, the harder it will be to cover it with climbing plants.

Maintenance of structures

Keep an eye on well-established climbers to be sure that they aren't damaging the building or structure that supports them. Gutters and drainpipes are particularly at risk as plant stems can wind around and distort them, and stems can also sneak under roof tiles. Self-clinging climbers pose no problems on sound, well-pointed walls, but keep growth trimmed away from window frames and other paintwork. Check panel and close-board fences every so often for stems that may creep through and enlarge any gaps.

Buying and choosing timber and fixings

DIY or kit form

Not only complete structures are available in kit form, but separate pieces can also be purchased ready-prepared to be incorporated into your own design. For example, it is possible to buy posts that are slotted ready to hold a cross-beam at the top, as well as rafters that are notched to sit on a pair of cross-beams, and shaped at the ends. Of course, this does tend to work out more expensive than doing it yourself; as a rough guide it can cost about half as much again. However, this obviously needs to be balanced against the amount of work it saves you and the professional finish achieved. Check your options first by looking at the product availability and prices at your garden centre and timber merchant. In any case it is worth shopping around as timber prices can vary considerably.

Sizes

Wood is sold according to metric sizes, with width and depth measured in millimetres and length in metres. For ease of understanding, the dimensions of the structures detailed in the projects are also given in inches and feet. However, when you come to buy your wood, be aware that if you order it by the foot you may be given it by the 'metric foot' – that is, 30 cm as opposed to 30.48 cm. In most cases this is not important, but if you are buying a large amount of wood it can make a significant difference: for instance, 10 'metric feet' is nearly 5 cm (2 in) shorter than 10 actual feet.

Type of wood

All the construction methods and measurements refer to sawn softwood which is the type most widely used for garden purposes. If you wish to use planed timber which has a smoother finish, bear in mind that the width and depth quoted are often those of the sawn wood before it is planed and hence the actual size is significantly smaller.

Hardwood looks very smart and lasts for a long time, but it is more expensive, and its strength makes the insertion of screws more difficult. If brass screws are used, it is preferable first to make channels for them using a steel screw.

Screws

The most widely used material for screws is mild steel, which rusts easily. For outdoor use it is best to use screws made of a non-rusting material such as brass or stainless steel.

The two basic screw head types are round-head and countersunk. Countersunk screws are generally better as they are less obtrusive. When screwing into softwood, tightening

the screw to pull the head into the wood may be sufficient, but to give a stronger joint it is preferable first to make a tapered hole for the head using a countersinking tool.

Before fixing a screw in place, it is necessary to drill holes for it in each of the two pieces of wood which are being joined together. Two different drill bits will be required: one to drill a narrow pilot hole which is a little shorter than the length of the screw, to go in the piece of wood which will take the lower, threaded part of the screw, and a shorter, wider clearance hole in the wood that will take the upper part. Check with your hardware or DIY store as to the correct drill sizes to match the gauge of your screws.

Staining and painting timber

All timber needs protection for it to withstand the weather and look good for a number of years. However, the only parts that are in real danger of rotting are those sections of timber that are in direct contact with the ground, which usually means the supporting posts. The only real long-lasting means of protection is pressure-treating them with preservative. This needs to be done professionally, and it's usual for fence posts already to have been treated in this way. Nonetheless, you should always double-check before buying.

~

Strong wire mesh makes an excellent support for light-weight climbers such as these annual sweet peas. It also has the bonus of needing very little maintenance.

Treated timber can then be stained or painted with the colour of your choice. Most timber for garden use is rough-sawn softwood, which will readily take up stains and preservatives but is more difficult to paint. Planed timber is more expensive and does not absorb liquid so readily, so the final colour tends to be several shades lighter than the rough-sawn timber treated with the same colour of stain. However, planed wood is easier to paint.

Stains and preservatives let the grain of the wood show through, which usually enhances the appearance of the overall structure as well as the wood itself, while paint takes much longer to apply and is more difficult to maintain, particularly in damp locations. The most widely available colour of wood stain and preservative is brown, with shades ranging from pale golden-brown to reddish tones and dark brown. Different colours such as green, blue, red and orange are available, though they tend to be at the expensive end of the product range.

Paint for garden structures must be suitable for outdoor use, which excludes emulsion paint. Gloss paint can be used, though as it is inflexible it does tend to crack and bubble up over time. Microporous paint is more durable as it contains acrylic resin, which makes the paint more flexible and allows water to escape.

Some stains and preservatives can be toxic to plants and animals, so it's a very good idea to take the surroundings into consideration when deciding which product to use. Creosote, a coal-tar-based product, is most toxic, and it also has a strong smell that can take months to disappear completely. Solvent-based products tend to be harmful to plants too. However, there are a number of stains now available which are said to be harmless to plants.

If the structure is in a shady area or it is liable to stay damp for long periods of time, it may also be worth painting the treated wood with a colourless preservative that will help prevent mould and algal growth. This product is applied after the timber has been treated with a normal stain or preservative and left to dry for 48 hours.

Whatever product you decide to use, be sure to follow the manufacturer's instructions. Apply the stain using a paintbrush and wear protective clothing including rubber gloves and some form of eye protection, because this liquid can easily be splashed about during application and can irritate the skin and eyes.

Preserving wooden structures in future years

Wood stain, preservative or paint will need to be reapplied every three to five years, usually once the colour fades but before the surface of the wood starts to deteriorate. If there are plants growing on or near the structure, take that into account when choosing your product as some materials are toxic (see above). Be sure to use a product that is safe for plants if there is any danger at all of splashing the foliage. Whatever product is used, it's advisable to tie the plant growth back and cover it with polythene to prevent any disfiguring splashes on the leaves.

The best time of year to carry out this work is in summer, as the wood should be completely dry and the stain or paint needs to be applied when there is no risk of rain. Clean the wood before treating it. Stained wood is best cleaned using a wire brush to clear off any dirt, mould or green algal growth. Painted wood needs to be rubbed down with sandpaper to remove any loose, flaking paint. Any soft, rotting patches of wood should be scraped out, and any holes or cracks filled with a proprietary wood filler. If it is necessary to use water to scrub off dirt, let the wood dry for at least 48 hours before treating it. Weathered timber which is old and dry tends to soak up lots of stain, so it is likely to need two or even three coats to obtain a good-looking and even finish.

If treating a fence, first check that it does belong to you to avoid any potential arguments with your neighbours. Bear in mind that you'll need to treat both sides in order for the preservative to be effective, and also because it's almost impossible to paint one side without ugly runs and drips coming through on the other side.

Choosing the right materials for your structure

When you come to choose the materials for your structure, don't forget to consider them in relation to any adjacent existing buildings and structures. For example, if you are building a brick-pillared pergola next to a house, it is best for the brick types to be as similar as possible to give a harmonious overall appearance. In a similar vein, an arch, pergola or arbour in an informal cottage garden may look best if built with rustic poles rather than sawn timber with its crisp, straight lines. When buying materials, remember that there are a number of reclamation merchants who often have old bricks and timber for sale, in addition to all the new timber and brick types available from builders merchants.

Metric/Imperial Conversion Chart

The following conversion formulae may be useful:

To convert to metric,
multiply by the factor shown

To convert from metric,
divide by the factor
Feet/metres – 0.3048
Inches/millimetres – 25.4
Inches/centimetres – 2.54

For example, to convert 12 ft to metres
the formula is:
12 x 0.3048 = 3.66 m

To convert 3.66 m to feet
the formula is:
3.6 ÷ 0.3048 = 12 ft

Project One

~

A double-sided pergola

Along pergola over a pathway makes a magnificent feature that can transform almost any part of the garden. In an open area, for example, it creates a whole new dimension with lots of visual interest in what would otherwise be a flat and featureless part of the garden. The crisp, straight lines of this design stand out in the landscape. Climbing plants soften the pergola just enough to blend it in with the surrounding borders.

There are several design variations that could be employed with a long pergola of this type. An attractive focal point such as an ornament or a seat could be sited at the far end, to tempt you to stroll through the pergola and onwards to explore the garden further. If you are lucky enough to have a good view from your garden, a pergola could be sited to frame and emphasize it. Alongside a house, a long pergola could be built over a pathway, and given a solid roof too if it was necessary to have sheltered access to another building such as a garage or a utility room.

~

*A wooden pergola turns an ordinary path into a
really special feature. A seat or statue could be
added at the end to create a focal point and draw
the visitor through the pergola.*

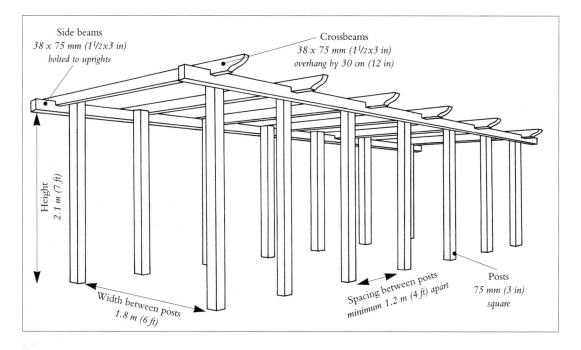

Side beams
*38 x 75 mm (1¹/2x3 in)
bolted to uprights*

Crossbeams
*38 x 75 mm (1¹/2x3 in)
overhang by 30 cm (12 in)*

Height
2.1 m (7 ft)

Width between posts
1.8 m (6 ft)

Spacing between posts
minimum 1.2 m (4 ft) apart

Posts
*75 mm (3 in)
square*

This pergola is made completely of wood and it is reasonably straightforward to construct. However, if you don't fancy making one from scratch, there are plenty of different pergola designs that come in kit form, all ready to be put together. With regard to dimensions, the pergola can be as long as you wish, though its size does need to be in keeping with that of the garden in order to retain a feeling of balance. The height should be no less than 2.1 m (7 ft) to give some headroom below the plant growth that will eventually dangle from the cross-beams. Allow a little more headroom if you plan to plant a wisteria that has extra-long racemes of flowers. The width can vary to fit that of the path, though it's best for it to be no less than 1.8 m (6 ft) wide in order to allow plenty of clearance from plant growth. The items listed below are sufficient to make a pergola 2.4 m (8 ft) wide and 7.3 m (24 ft) long.

Constructing the pergola

1. Cut the timber to the required lengths. Your supplier may do this for a small additional charge, which can save a lot of work. Treat any cut ends with wood preservative, paying special attention to the parts that will be in contact with the ground.

2. Using a tape measure and measuring lines mark out the sites for the posts, spacing them 1.2 m (4 ft) apart.

3. Drill holes for the bolts in the side beams and the upright posts, allowing for two bolts to each upright. It's much easier to do this before the uprights go up, particularly if you drill the side beam first and then mark the corresponding places to be drilled on the upright. However, be sure to make a note of which upright matches which pair of holes by marking them with chalk.

MATERIALS

14 posts 75 mm (3 in) square and a minimum 2.1 m (7 ft) high
(If sinking the posts into the ground, add an extra 60 cm (2 ft) to each one)

Metal spikes or concrete in which to set the posts (see page 26 for options)

6 crossbeams 38 x 75 mm (1½ x 3 in) and 3.3 m (11 ft) long

38 x 75 mm (1½ x 3 in) timber for the 2 side beams, total length 15.6 m (51 ft)

28 bolts, length 12.5 cm (5 in), with nuts and washers, for fixing the side beams to the posts

28 galvanized nails, length 6 cm (2½ in) for fixing the crossbeams to the side beams.
(An alternative to notching and nailing the crossbeams is to sit each one in a U-shaped galvanized metal bracket)

Wood stain or preservative (see page 19)

TOOLS

Spirit level

Tape measure and measuring lines

Electric drill with bit of the same diameter as the bolts

Saw and chisel for notching the side beams

Hammer

Stepladder

Paint brush

Protective clothing

Chalk

4. Put up the upright posts (see options overleaf), checking each one carefully on both sides with a spirit level to be sure it is absolutely upright. This is very important as even a slight lean can put the whole structure out of line.

5. Working from the stepladder, fix the side beams to the posts, screwing the bolt through the side beam and the upright and holding it firm with a nut and washer on the other end. At each end of the pergola the side beams can protrude about 30 cm (12 in) from the uprights. For safety's sake, do make sure that the fixings are very secure as they will take the whole weight of the timber and any future plant growth. This job is safer and much easier if you have a second person to steady the ladder and to hand up bits and pieces to you.

6. Sit the crossbeams in position and mark the areas where the notches are to be cut out. Notch the undersides by cutting about a third of the way through the wood. If you wish, shape the ends of the crossbeams for a more decorative finish such as in the diagram on page 24. Treat the cut surfaces with wood preservative and allow it to dry.

7. Set the notched crossbeams on top of the side beams and nail them in place, leaving a gap of about 1.2m (4 ft) between each beam. If you don't fancy the job of notching, simply set the crossbeams on top of the side beams and hold them in place with U-shaped metal brackets. These brackets are fixed to the side beams and the crossbeams simply sit in the U of the bracket.

Erecting posts

Structurally the posts are the most important part of the feature, so it's important to ensure that they are erected securely. The posts will not only support the whole of the structure itself, but also the mass of plant growth that will clothe the feature and will create a lot of wind resistance too. Outlined below are several different ways of erecting the posts. Bear in mind that the section of post that goes into the ground is really the only part of the structure susceptible to rotting, so the better the wood is protected, the longer it will last.

I strongly recommend buying posts that have been professionally pressure-treated with preservative so that the wood lasts as long as possible. If for any reason you have to cut the ends of the posts, soak the cut ends in wood preservative for at least 24 hours before use (large cut-down, plastic mineral-water bottles are ideal for this job).

Method 1 Directly in the ground

The simplest method is to make a hole 45–60 cm (18–24 in) deep in the ground and put the post in it. However, the great disadvantage is that the whole bottom section of the post is in direct contact with damp soil, which makes it liable to rot and break off within a few years. This method is also unsuitable for sandy, stony or otherwise loose soils where concrete or metal spikes will be needed to give the post stability.

Rather than digging the hole with a spade, which takes out far more soil and makes more work than is necessary, use a soil drill –

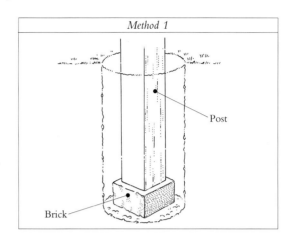

Method 1

Post

Brick

usually called a post-hole borer – which removes a narrow core of soil. It can be obtained from most tool-hire shops for a very reasonable charge. Then take out any loose debris from the bottom of the hole and check with a cane or similar marker that it is of the exact depth required. Put in a half-brick or a level lump of concrete to make a firm base for the post. Put the post in the hole and use the spirit level to check that it is absolutely upright on both sides, then backfill the hole with soil. Ram the loose soil down firmly using a large piece of wood such as another fence post, ideally with a second person holding the post and the spirit level to be sure that it remains upright throughout.

Method 2 In concrete

Encasing the post in a concrete 'sleeve' will extend its life considerably. Again, a post-hole borer is useful to make a narrow hole that will use much less concrete than one that is dug with a spade. Make the hole to the same depth as above, and use a spade to trim the sides to about 20 cm (8 in) square. Again,

These ornamental gourds make an exceptionally unusual display on a long pergola. The fruits can be harvested and used for winter decoration indoors too.

~

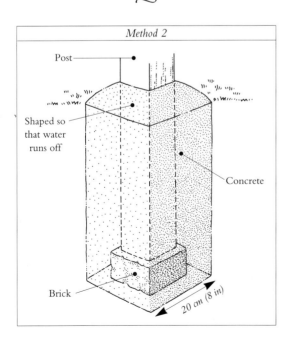

Method 2

Post

Shaped so that water runs off

Concrete

Brick

20 cm (8 in)

put a half–brick or concrete in the base. On light or stony soils that are liable to crumble easily it may be necessary to line the sides with pieces of timber to shutter the concrete, extending the ends about 5 cm (2 in) above ground level.

For the concrete, use a mixture of 1 part cement to 2.5 parts sand and 4 parts coarse aggregate or gravel. With a spade, mix all the dry ingredients until the mixture is a uniform colour. If you have only a small number of posts to put up, it is easier to buy bags of pre–mixed material, but this is more expensive on a larger scale. Slowly add water to the dry mix, using the spade to turn the material thoroughly until it is firm and workable but not runny. Make up only as much concrete as you can use within an hour as it will soon begin to dry and harden.

Put the post in the hole and fill the gap

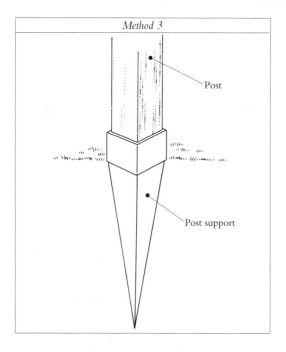

Method 3

Post

Post support

damp a lot of the time. However, replacing a post in a metal socket is much easier than if it has been set in concrete.

These spikes come in various sizes. For all but the smallest structures choose spikes that are at least 60 cm (24 in) long. You'll also need a special metal tool which sits in the socket while you are banging the spike into the ground with a sledgehammer. Use the spirit level to check that the socket is exactly vertical. Once the spike is fully buried in the ground with the socket still above ground level, remove the metal tool and fit the post into the socket, checking again to be sure that it is absolutely upright. If the ground is very loose or stony, it's a good idea to set the spikes in concrete for added stability.

Method 4 Using a bolt-down socket (for a concrete surface)

If your ground is already covered with concrete, there are bolt-down post sockets that can be fixed to it. Holes for the bolts need to be drilled with an electric drill fitted with a masonry bit, and then the socket is secured with strong masonry bolts.

with concrete, then ram it down with a piece of wood to get rid of any air spaces. Use a spirit level to check that the post is absolutely upright. Extend the concrete to just above ground level to make a collar for the post, and slope the top of the concrete away from the post so that rainwater will run straight off instead of sitting around the wood. Allow several days for the concrete to set thoroughly before carrying on with the construction.

Method 3 Using a spiked steel post support

Using a spiked steel post support is a quicker and easier option than concrete. A steel support is designed with a long spike topped with a square socket to hold the end of the post. From the point of durability this method tends to fall between the two outlined previously because the base of the post can stay

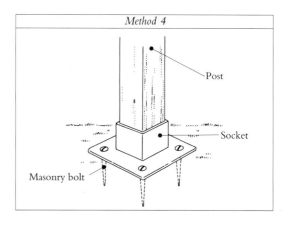

Method 4

Post

Socket

Masonry bolt

Plants for the pergola

A large pergola offers stacks of potential for plants, and there is plenty of space here for a selection of plants that will give colour and interest through the seasons. If the pergola occupies a prominent position or is on view from the house all year, it's a good idea to have evergreens or winter-flowering plants making up about a third of all the climbers, otherwise you'll be left with the bare bones of the pergola for nearly half the year. Should it be sited away from the house so that it is rarely seen in winter, concentrate on a bonanza of colour from late spring to autumn. All climbers, even self-clinging ones, will need support such as wires or netting in order to grow up the posts (see page 11).

Starting with plants for the depths of winter, many of the small-leaved ivies with variegated foliage will look really handsome and provide lots of cheerful colour in the darkest months. The same goes for *Jasminum nudiflorum* (winter jasmine) which can easily be trained up a post to smother it with bright yellow, starry flowers from early to late winter.

Earliest to flower of the spring clematis are *C. alpina* and *C. macropetala* with fresh green foliage and lovely, nodding heads of flowers. Later in the season *Wisteria* makes a truly breathtaking display of blooms provided it can have a sunny and sheltered position.

Then, moving into summer, honeysuckle is a fragrant delight, with *Lonicera periclymenum* 'Belgica' (early Dutch honeysuckle) being the first one to bloom. Another wonderful plant for scent is *Jasminum officinale* (summer jasmine), which bears clusters of white flowers. Rambler roses make a superb explosion of summer blossom, and there is ample room for them to fling their long, flower-laden branches over the top of the pergola. Large-flowered hybrid clematis make ideal partners for roses. One of the more vigorous hybrids would do well here where they can grow up to 3–3.6 m (10–12 ft). They include 'Edith' (pure white), 'Ernest Markham' (red), 'Gipsy Queen', 'Jackmanii Superba' (violet- purple) or 'Mrs Cholmondeley' (lavender-blue).

Clematis can hold sway in autumn too, this time the smaller-flowered species such as *C. viticella* and its hybrids in many colours, and *C. tangutica* with its harvest-gold lanterns of flowers. Deciduous plants with handsome foliage are certainly worth including for their long period of interest from spring to autumn, and some of them finish the season in a blaze of glorious autumn colour. They include *Parthenocissus henryana*, whose dark, silver-veined leaves change to fiery red before falling, and *Vitis coignetiae* with its huge, lobed leaves that turn many shades of red and orange in autumn.

Annual climbers are immensely useful for dressing a new structure during the first couple of years while the permanent plants become established. Sweet peas are always popular and in the picture on page 23 they have been widely used to clothe this new pergola with fragrant flowers. *Cobaea scandens* is another good annual as it is quick-growing and will soon twine along the crossbeams to give good display in late summer.

~

A brick-pillared pergola over a patio

One of the most pleasant purposes of a pergola is to provide a patch of dappled shade in which to sit, and what could be better than combining a pergola with a sunny patio? Here it is possible to sit in a warm, sheltered spot, yet with the fiercest of the sun's rays filtered out by the stout overhead beams and the climbing plants that twine and ramble over the top. Conveniently close to the house, it's an ideal place for an alfresco meal or a drink with friends, reading a book or just stretching out on a garden lounger and relaxing.

This pergola has been designed with two solidly built brick pillars to create a long-lasting structure that blends the house in well with the garden. On one side the wooden beams are supported by the brick pillars, and on the other side against the house (not shown in the photograph) by a notched wooden beam bolted to the wall. Of course, this design can be varied to suit your requirements; for example, by using brick pillars on all four corners instead of one side only, or

~

A brick-pillared pergola is a substantial and handsome structure, though it does take more skill to construct than one made of wood.

MATERIALS

260 bricks (120 for each pillar plus a
10 per cent allowance for wastage)

Hardcore for the foundation base

Sand, cement and aggregate to make the
concrete foundation (3 x 50 kg bags of ready-
prepared coarse dry mix would be adequate
for the amount needed here rather than
buying the ingredients separately)

Wood for shuttering the concrete

5 bags of pre-mixed mortar

2 bolts, length 25 cm (10 in) with nuts,
for fixing the side beams to the brick pillars

2 metal plates, diameter approx.
23 cm (9 in)

5 expanding masonry bolts, length 12.5 cm
(5 in) for fixing one supporting beam
to the house wall

75 x 100 mm (3 x 4 in) timber for the
2 side beams, total length 7.3 m (23 ft 6 in)

50 x 150 mm (2 x 6 in) timber for
supporting beam against the house wall,
2.7 m (9 ft) long

5 crossbeams 50 x 100 mm (2 x 4 in) and
2.7 m (9 ft) long

Approx. 40 nails, length 5 cm (2 in)

Wood stain or preservative (see page 19)

TOOLS

Spade or shovel for the mortar

Builder's float

Trowel and jointing tool

Marker lines

Plumb line and
set square or builder's square

Tape measure

Old fence post for tamping down soil

Saw, hammer, chisel

Screwdriver

Spirit level

Stepladder

Paint brush

Protective clothing

Electric drill with bits of the same diameter
as both sets of bolts

that stouter timbers and longer masonry bolts will be necessary. In this case consult your timber merchant for details.

Constructing the pergola

Note. There is a time lapse after preparation of the foundation, and again after building the pillars, in order to allow the concrete and mortar to harden. However, preparing the overheads and erecting the supporting beam against the house wall can be done during this time.

1. The brick pillars must have a firm foundation of hardcore and concrete (see Diagram 1).

by using timber posts as in project 1. The choice of materials obviously depends on the effect you want to create and the amount of time and money you wish to spend on making your pergola.

The size of this pergola is 2.4 x 3.6 m (8 x 12 ft). Should you wish to build a pergola to the same design on a larger scale, it is possible

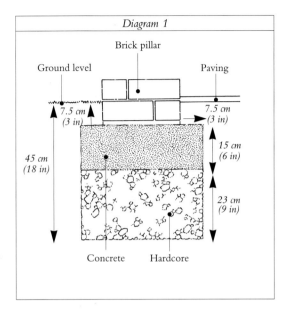

Diagram 1

Brick pillar

Ground level

Paving

7.5 cm (3 in)

7.5 cm (3 in)

45 cm (18 in)

15 cm (6 in)

23 cm (9 in)

Concrete   Hardcore

Mark out the sites for the foundations using a tape measure and two measuring lines. To prepare the foundations first dig out the site for the base to a depth of 45 cm (18 in), making it about 7.5 cm (3 in) wider all round than the actual size of the pillar. Tamp down any loose soil in the base with a large piece of wood such as an old fence post. Half-fill the hole with hardcore such as pieces of broken bricks and tamp it down firmly. Put pieces of wood around the sides of the hole to shutter

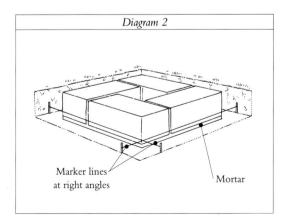

Diagram 2

Marker lines at right angles

Mortar

the concrete. Mix up the concrete as described on page 27 and fill the hole to within 7.5 cm (3 in) of ground level, taking care to push it well into the corners so that there are no gaps or air spaces. Using a builder's float, smooth off the top and use a spirit level to check that it is level. Leave the concrete for a week to harden fully, removing the shuttering after a couple of days.

2. Once the foundation has hardened completely, the pillars can be built. First set out two marker lines at right angles, checking with a set square or builder's square that the angle is exact as it is vital that the first bricks are laid in the correct position. Mix up a batch of mortar, preparing only as much as you can use within an hour or so or it will start to harden. Put a layer of mortar about 2.5 cm (1 in) thick on the foundation, pick up the first brick, 'butter' one end with a layer of mortar and lay it on the base layer of

~

Note on bricklaying
Bricklaying is a skilled occupation, although an amateur can achieve an acceptable finish with a little practice. If this is your first attempt at bricklaying, it is worth reading one of the many DIY books on the subject and then getting some old bricks on which to practise in an out-of-the-way part of the garden where failure would not be a disaster.

~

Winter jasmine can easily be trained up the pillars of a pergola, and its bright yellow blooms brighten the darkest months of the year.

~

mortar (see Diagram 2). Check with a spirit level that it is level. Pick up the next brick, 'butter' it as before and lay it, butting it up closely to the first one. Lay the remaining two bricks to complete the first layer.

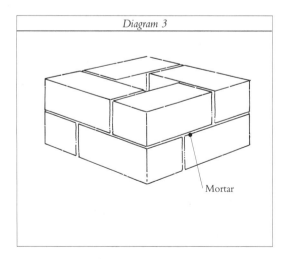

Diagram 3

Mortar

3. Continue to build the pillar in this way with the brick joints overlapping (see Diagram 3), frequently checking both the horizontal and vertical levels with the spirit level and the plumb line. The mortar joints should be about 12 mm (½ in) thick. After every couple of courses of bricks have been laid, point the mortar for a smoother finish. It may be necessary to add a little mortar in order to get a clean, smooth joint.

4. Before laying the top two courses of bricks (each pillar consists of 30 courses) drill a hole in the centre of each metal plate to match the 25 cm (10 in) bolts. Put the bolt through the plate so that it points upwards with the head underneath. Then set the plate in the centre of the pillar, on the layer of mortar that is ready to receive the next course of bricks (see Diagram 4) and cement it in place. It's a good

~

Rambler roses are superb plants for pergolas. This variety is 'Goldfinch', with clusters of delicately scented flowers.

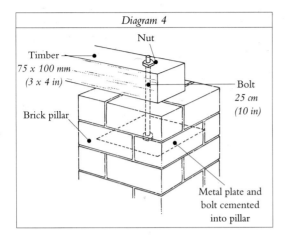

Diagram 4

Nut

Timber
75 x 100 mm
(3 x 4 in)

Bolt
25 cm
(10 in)

Brick pillar

Metal plate and
bolt cemented
into pillar

idea to drill the plates before starting to build the pillars, so that you can construct them without interruption. Lay the final two courses of bricks. Leave the pillars for at least three or four days so that the mortar hardens fully.

5. Prepare and put up the supporting beam against the house wall. It is vital that this beam is securely fixed with expanding masonry bolts. Before putting the beam up, drill holes for the bolts in both the beam and the house wall, allowing for one bolt at each end of the beam and three in between. Use a saw, hammer and chisel to cut two notches about 5 cm (2 in) deep near the ends, to hold the other two outer support-ing beams (see Diagram 5). Make sure that these notches and the beam are aligned with the brick pillars. Enlist two people to hold the house-wall beam while you bolt it into place, ensuring that the bottoms of the notches are at the same level. Take great care that it and the other outer beams are securely fixed in place, as they support all the remaining overheads in the structure as well as any future plant growth.

6. The two outer beams of the pergola (marked A and B in Diagram 6) can now be put up. First, in one end of both beams, drill a hole for the bolts that are protruding from the top of the brick pillars (see Diagram 4). Then with a second person helping, lift each beam into place. Screw the nuts firmly on to the ends of the bolts.

7. Prepare the five crossbeams by using a saw, hammer and chisel to cut notches about half-way through each end so that they sit securely on the supporting outer beams (see Diagram 5). To achieve a smooth finish it may be easier to make several cuts with the saw so that the wood in the notch can be chiselled out in small pieces. If necessary, use a file to smooth off the base of the notch.

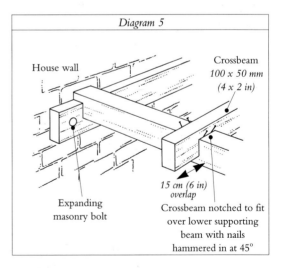

Diagram 5

House wall

Crossbeam
100 x 50 mm
(4 x 2 in)

15 cm (6 in)
overlap

Expanding
masonry bolt

Crossbeam notched to fit
over lower supporting
beam with nails
hammered in at 45°

Alternatively it is possible to buy ready-notched pergola beams. Paint any bare surfaces with wood preservative and allow it to dry. The ends should protrude about 15 cm (6 in) beyond the two outer supporting beams, and they can be shaped for extra dec-

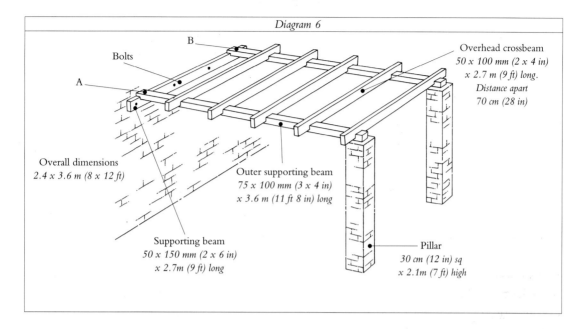

Diagram 6

B

Bolts

Overhead crossbeam
*50 x 100 mm (2 x 4 in)
x 2.7 m (9 ft) long.
Distance apart
70 cm (28 in)*

A

Overall dimensions
2.4 x 3.6 m (8 x 12 ft)

Outer supporting beam
*75 x 100 mm (3 x 4 in)
x 3.6 m (11 ft 8 in) long*

Supporting beam
*50 x 150 mm (2 x 6 in)
x 2.7m (9 ft) long*

Pillar
*30 cm (12 in) sq
x 2.1m (7 ft) high*

orative effect if desired (as in the photograph on page 39). Set the crossbeams in place spaced an equal distance apart – about 70 cm (28 in) – then fix them on to the supporting beams by hammering in nails at an angle of about 45 degrees.

Plants for the pergola

A sunny site that is given extra shelter by the storage-heater effect of the house is perfect for growing an exciting and exotic selection of climbers in all but the coldest areas. *Campsis* (trumpet flower) needs a sun-baked spot to produce a lavish display of large, rich yellow or glowing orange blooms, and its bold, fresh green leaves are handsome too. This vigorous climber will soon spread across the roof of a pergola, as will *Passiflora caerulea* (passion flower),

which has attractive, lobed leaves and stunning blue or white blooms. After a long, hot summer, there is often a bonus in the form of large orange fruits that are shown off beautifully against the dark green leaves.

Against the house wall, *Trachelospermum* is a useful evergreen, self-clinging climber with jasmine-like flowers that are gloriously scented. Last but not least, *Wisteria* thrives in a sheltered spot, and its racemes of scented flowers hang down from the beams to make a breathtaking display in late spring.

For a shady site, good climbers include shade-loving honeysuckles such as *Lonicera* x *tellmanniana* and *L. tragophylla,* which have glorious yellow flowers; *Parthenocissus* and *Vitis* species have extremely handsome foliage, while *Jasminum nudiflorum* (winter jasmine) can be trained up the pillars to provide a cheering display of yellow blossom even in the very depths of winter.

Project Three

~

A beamed arbour

There is something wonderfully indulgent about having a secluded place to sit in the garden, particularly when it contains an enticing seat in fragrant shade. Although the patio is the obvious place to sit, it's good to have an alternative, either to follow the path of the sun around the garden or just to have somewhere you can retreat to admire the view from a different perspective.

All but the smallest gardens could have a timbered arbour of this type, especially as its size can easily be varied to suit the site. Here the arbour is square, supported by four stout posts that are taller than average so that they clear the ground-floor windows of the house. Alternative adaptations could be to extend it to a rectangular design, or to tuck it snugly into a corner by using three posts only and running the overhead timbers diagonally to form a triangle.

The protruding ends of the overhead beams have been shaped by making a long, slanting cut on the underside of each one. The timbers should be cut before they go up. Your timber merchant may be prepared to do the job for a small extra charge. Alternatively buy ready-shaped and notched beams. The items listed here are sufficient for an arbour measuring 2.4 m (8 ft) square.

MATERIALS

4 posts 100 mm (4 in) square to stand a minimum of 2.1 m (7 ft) above ground

Metal spikes or concrete in which to set the posts (see page 26 for options)

8 beams 50 x 100 mm (2 x 4 in) and 2.4 m (8 ft) long

8 crossbraces 25 mm (1 in) square and 30 cm (12 in) long

8 brass screws, length 6 cm (2½ in)

12 brass screws, length 7.5 cm (3 in)

16 galvanized nails, length 5 cm (2 in)

Woodstain or preservative (see page 19)

TOOLS

Electric drill with bits of the same diameter as the above screws

Spirit level, saw, hammer, screwdriver

Chisel and file

Tape measure and measuring lines

Stepladder

Chalk or pencil and protractor

Paint brush, protective clothing

~

This wooden arbour is clothed with honeysuckle to turn it into a wonderfully fragrant retreat for sitting and relaxing.

Constructing the arbour

1. In the tops of each of the four posts, cut notches approximately 5 cm (2 in) wide and deep to match the overhead beams that will be set in these notches (see Diagram 2 for detail). Do this by making the two vertical cuts with a saw the width of the notch, and two cuts in between, then use the hammer and chisel to cut through the bottom of these pieces to be removed.

If necessary, use a file to smooth off the base of the notch as it must be level, or the beam that will sit in it may lie crookedly. Paint the cut surfaces with wood preservative and allow it to dry. Alternatively buy posts which are ready-notched.

2. Using a tape measure and measuring lines mark out the sites for the posts 2.1 m (7 ft)

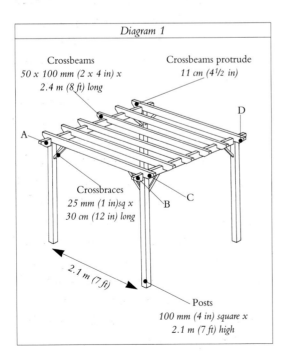

Diagram 1

Crossbeams
50 x 100 mm (2 x 4 in) x 2.4 m (8 ft) long

Crossbeams protrude
11 cm (4½ in)

A

D

Crossbraces
25 mm (1 in)sq x 30 cm (12 in) long

B

C

2.1 m (7 ft)

Posts
100 mm (4 in) square x 2.1 m (7 ft) high

apart and put them up according to your chosen option (see page 26), checking both sides with the spirit level to be sure that they are upright.

It may sound obvious, but do make sure that the notches in the tops are all facing the same way! The tops of the posts should all be exactly the same height too. This can be checked by lying one of the beams on top of two posts and putting the spirit level on the beam.

3. Lift the two side beams (marked A and B in Diagram 1) into place, setting each end securely in the notches on the ends of the posts. Drill holes (one on each side of the notch) horizontally through the tops of the upright posts and side beams, then fix the beams securely in place with 6 cm (2½ in) screws.

4. Notch the undersides of both ends of all the crossbeams so that they will sit on beams A and B. The notches should be 5 cm (2 in) wide and deep. The ends of these beams should protrude about 11 cm (4½ in) beyond the lower ones. Use chalk or pencil to mark where the cuts should go.

If you wanted to skip the job of notching these six crossbeams, you can secure them instead using galvanized metal U-shaped brackets or metal right-angles.

5. Put up the beams at each end (marked C and D in Diagram 1). Fix them to beams A and B by drilling through the top into the lower beam, then securing the two together using 7.5 cm (3 in) screws.

6. Now the four outer beams are in place, the crossbraces can be put up. First shape the ends by sawing them off at an angle of 45

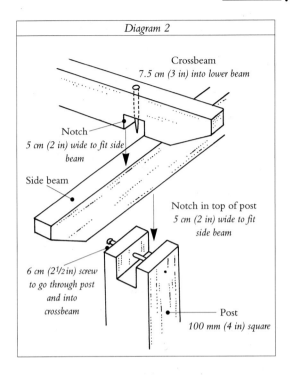

Diagram 2

Crossbeam
7.5 cm (3 in) into lower beam

Notch
5 cm (2 in) wide to fit side
beam

Side beam

Notch in top of post
5 cm (2 in) wide to fit
side beam

6 cm (2½ in) screw
to go through post
and into
crossbeam

Post
100 mm (4 in) square

degrees (use a protractor to measure this), so that each one fits snugly against the post at one end and the crossbeam the other. Treat these cut ends with wood preservative and allow it to dry. Nail the braces in place using one 5 cm (2 in) nail at each end.

7. The remaining four crossbeams can now be put up. First set them all on beams A and B, but don't fix them in place until you're satisfied that the spacing between them is identical. The gap should be approximately 30 cm (15 in). Finally screw them in place as step 5 opposite.

Fragrant plants for the arbour

Being surrounded by drifts of scent helps to intensify the feeling of relaxation, and there is no shortage of deliciously fragrant plants from which to choose. The honeysuckle clothing the arbour in the photograph is *Lonicera japonica* 'Halliana' a vigorous, semi-evergreen variety with masses of small, scented flowers. Most other honeysuckles have fragrant flowers too, with the exception of *L. x tell-manniana*, *L. tragophylla* and *L. x brownii* 'Dropmore Scarlet'. An easily grown old favourite is *Jasminum officinale* (summer jasmine), with clusters of pure white flowers.

Less common is *Akebia quinata*, a pretty, scrambling climber with small, fresh green, lobed leaves and rich, dark red flowers borne in late spring. The flowers are not exceptionally ornamental, but they have a lovely sweet scent.

For a sheltered spot *Trachelospermum* has deliciously fragrant, jasmine-like flowers, while *Wisteria* makes a splendid display in late spring. Both of these plants take a few years to mature, while annual sweet peas give a quick and superb show of scented flowers.

Roses are invaluable for mid-summer scent, and it's well worth paying a visit to a rose garden or a specialist nursery when they are in bloom to choose your fragrant favourites for autumn delivery. Good older-style climbers and ramblers to look for include 'Easlea's Golden Rambler' (yellow), 'Guinée' (deep crimson), 'Madame Alfred Carrière' (white/blush pink), 'Sombreuil' (creamy-white), 'Weetwood' (pale pink) and 'Zéphirine Drouhin' (deep pink). Fragrant modern climbers, with flowers that resemble a hybrid tea rose, include 'Compassion' (salmon-pink), 'Pink Perpétué' (deep pink) and 'Schoolgirl' (apricot).

Project Four

~

A trellis screen

Without a doubt trellis is the best all-purpose material for creating a vertical garden. Quick to put up, easy to handle and available in an enormous range of sizes and styles, trellis can be used to make all sorts of different structures.

One of its prime uses is as a screen, either on the garden boundary or as a divider within the garden itself, where it creates privacy without the claustrophobia that can be induced by a solid barrier. It can also do sterling service in hiding the jumble of practical items such as compost heaps, tools and pots which is part of the everyday life of most gardeners.

Another beauty of trellis is the range of styles to match just about every budget. There are simple square and diamond-patterned panels, which come in sizes from 30 cm x 1.8 m (1 x 6 ft) to 1.8 x 1.8 m (6 x 6 ft). Then, going up the price range, there are lots of different decorative designs, including panels that can be combined for an undulating, wave-topped effect, some with concave or curving tops, and panels that

~

Dividing a small garden with a trellis screen can actually make it appear larger, by creating more interest and variety.

42

MATERIALS

2 trellis panels 1.5 m x 1.8 m (5 x 6 ft)

1 trellis panel 90 cm x 1.8 m (3 x 6 ft)

5 trellis panels 60 cm x 1.8 m (2 x 6 ft)

12 fence posts 75 mm (3 in) square to stand 2.1 m (7ft) above ground

Metal spikes or concrete in which to set the posts (see page 26 for options)

Timber 38 x 75 mm (1½ x 3 in) for the overhead framework in the following lengths (to match the widths of the trellis panels above), 4 at 1.5 m (5 ft); 4 at 1.2 m (4 ft); 2 at 90 cm (3 ft); 6 at 60 cm (2 ft)

12 post caps and finials (post caps alone can be used if you need to limit costs)

12 brass screws, length 11 cm (4½ in)

40 galvanized metal right-angled brackets

24 galvanized nails, length 2.5 cm (1 in)

48 galvanized nails, length 11 cm (4½ in)

Paint or woodstain (see page 19)

TOOLS

Hammer

Screwdriver

Electric drill with bits of the same diameter as the screws, plus one drill bit of a slightly smaller diameter than the nails

Stepladder

Spirit level

Tape measure and measuring line

Paint brush

Protective clothing

have a 'window' in the centre. There are also styles that fall part-way between trellis and fencing, made with rustic timber in an open pattern.

The stylish little garden shown in the photograph on page 42 illustrates perfectly how a small plot can actually appear larger if it is broken up into sections by a trellis screen. The screen adds interest to the overall design too, because of the slight air of mystery that is created by the fact that the garden cannot all be seen at once. This screen turns the far end of the garden into a pleasant and secluded spot whence the plot can be admired from a different perspective. Note the white-washed walls, the pale colour of which helps further to increase the feeling of space.

However, it's not necessary to buy expensive trellis in order to create an extremely decorative effect. Look closely at this screen and you'll see that it is made of panels of ordinary, square trellis which have been combined with a wooden framework to make a handsome and exceptionally effective feature. Painted white, and with the addition of some rounded finials to give a lovely finishing touch, this feature could add a touch of real style to any garden without costing an arm and a leg.

The width of the screen can obviously be varied to suit your own garden, but it is best for the gaps for the pathway to remain at least 1.2 m (4 ft) wide to give adequate space to walk through with barrows or other loads. The items listed on the left are sufficient for a trellis screen measuring 6.75 m (22 ft) wide and 75 cm (2½ ft deep).

Note. An alternative to fixing the overhead timbers with screws and metal brackets is to cut joints for them in the uprights and secure them in place with wood glue. However, this is time-consuming as there would be a large number of joints to cut. If choosing this option, allow an extra 5–7.5 cm (2–3 in) on each piece of timber for the framework. Another option is to use wooden dowels and wood glue to join the timbers together. Both these options take more time and skill, but give a neater finish.

Constructing the trellis screen

1. Using a tape measure and measuring lines mark out the sites for the posts, running the measuring line across the width of the

garden, and put them up according to your chosen method. When marking out, bear in mind that the measurements shown in the diagram refer to the area between the posts, so remember to allow for the width of each post too. It's best to use the trellis panels themselves to measure the spaces required, as the sizes of the panels may vary a little.

2. Fix the overhead beams to the posts, leaving about 15 cm (6 in) of post protruding above the beams. (This is purely for decorative effect: the overheads can be put up flush with the tops of the posts if desired.) The 60 cm (2 ft) crosspieces are fixed with 11 cm (4½ in) brass screws. Drill through each post and into the timber, then fix the screw in place. Use the spirit level to check that the timbers are level. The remaining overheads are secured with

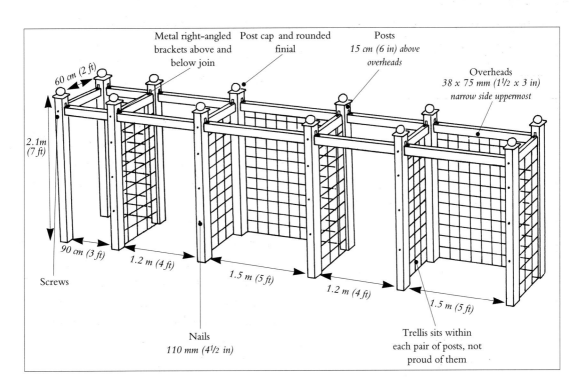

45

This deep blue Clematis 'Mrs Cholmondeley' makes a marvellous contrast to white trellis.

~

right-angled brackets, one above and one below each joint. This job needs to be done from a stepladder, and it's a great help to have someone holding the ladder and passing up wood and tools.

3. Prepare to nail the trellis panels to the posts using the 11 cm (4½ in) galvanized nails, six to each panel. The nails need to be hammered through the posts and into the border of each panel, but to avoid knocking the posts out of alignment, it's a good idea to drill holes for the nails first with a drill bit that is slightly smaller than the size of the nail. The panels should sit snugly in between the posts, rather than being nailed to one side or the other.

~

Rustic poles can be used to construct an open framework, an attractive alternative to small-meshed trellis.

4. Fix the finials to the flat post caps using one 2.5-cm (1-in) nail to each one, then nail the caps complete with finials on to the tops of the posts. The caps stop rainwater from sitting on the post tops and rotting them, and the finials add a decorative touch that really finishes off the whole feature.

5. Finally, stain or paint the entire structure to the colour of your choice (see page 19 for options).

Plants for the trellis screen

Whether to emphasize or conceal is the first question to resolve when choosing plants for trellis. If you've spent a small fortune on stylish designer trellis, it's unlikely that you'll want to smother it with rampant plants so that it disappears from view. Likewise a decorative garden-divider of the type featured here benefits from a minimum of planting. However, where you are using trellis to give privacy, vigorous plants will be required.

Compact plants for decorative trellis

Annual climbers are valuable for providing rapid cover over a long period of time, and their thin stems do little to obscure the overall structure. Most annuals need a reasonable amount of sun; sweet peas flourish on a deep, retentive soil, and *Ipomoea* (morning glory) needs full sun to bring out a good display of its exquisite blue trumpets. Both these and the dark, black-purple flowers of *Rhodochiton atrosanguineus* (purple bell vine) would look particularly good on white trellis.

Of the less vigorous perennial climbers, those with attractive foliage include *Lonicera japonica* 'Aureoreticulata' whose leaves are prettily variegated with gold, the variegated forms of *Jasminum officinale* (summer jasmine), and *Actinidia kolomikta* with pink-, cream-and-green leaves. Large flowered hybrid clematis that are fairly compact include 'Asao' (deep pink), 'Daniel Deronda' (purple), 'Guernsey Cream' (creamy yellow) and 'Silver Moon' (pale mauve).

Herbaceous climbers are useful as they rarely get a chance to swamp their supports, *Humulus lupulus* 'Aureus' (golden hop) is a vigorous creature but a forgiving one that will tolerate chunks being hacked off its rootstock if it starts to take over. Its lobed, golden leaves look lovely in their own right as well as complementing a host of different flowers, and it does well in sun or part-shade.

Wall shrubs can easily be trained closely against a trellis screen. Handsome ones for a sunny site include abutilons with brightly coloured, bell-shaped flowers, *Aloysia triphylla* (lemon verbena) with delightfully aromatic leaves, *Escallonia* 'Gold Brian' and 'Gold Ellen' with deep old-gold foliage, and *Phygelius* (Cape figwort) with tall stems of exotic-looking flowers.

Where there is little sun, opt for *Chaenomeles* (flowering quince), one of the earliest shrubs to flower, and *Euonymus fortunei* varieties with evergreen foliage in a range of handsome variegations. Ivies (*Hedera helix* varieties) are excellent standbys for any situation and they can be easily trimmed to keep their growth within bounds.

Plants for privacy

In this case the need is to choose plants that will grow reasonably fast while avoiding those which are most vigorous as they would eventually swamp the trellis completely. Small-leaved ivies (*Hedera helix* cultivars) are excellent for screening as they are evergreen, as is *Lonicera japonica* 'Halliana'. Still with evergreens, *Pyracantha* can be trained closely against trellis: attach the main shoots horizontally and prune back any outward-facing ones in late spring.

Clematis species such as *C. orientalis* and *C. tangutica* are quick-growing, and their lanterns of golden flowers look superb in late summer. *Cotoneaster horizontalis* (herring-bone cotoneaster) doesn't take long to form a dense thicket of stems, and with spring flowers followed by autumn berries and attractive leaf colour, it really earns its place in the garden.

If privacy is only an issue for the summer months – if the trellis is screening a patio or seating area, for example – there are plenty of vigorous deciduous climbers that can be used. *Jasminum officinale* (summer jasmine) soon forms a dense mass of dark green foliage spangled with clusters of fragrant white flowers, while *Passiflora caerulea* (passion flower) has attractive lobed leaves and beautiful, unusually shaped blooms; the variety 'Constance Elliott' has pure white flowers that look extremely handsome. *Akebia quinata* is a little less vigorous, though it is a worthwhile addition with its attractive leaves and dark red, scented flowers. To fill any gaps, the vigorous annual climber *Tropaeolum peregrinum* (canary creeper) quickly grows from spring-sown seed to form a mass of small lobed leaves that make a lovely background to its fringed, yellow flowers.

Edible plants for trellis

Provided the site is reasonably sunny, it is even possible to clothe the trellis with edible plants. Trained fruit trees can make a very attractive screen and what could be nicer than a beautiful display of spring blossom followed by the sight of a crop of fruit gradually maturing to perfection.

The two shapes to look for are fans and espaliers. Apples and pears are available in both forms while plums, cherries, apricots, peaches and nectarines are sold as fans. The latter three trees need a very sunny and sheltered site, preferably in the mildest areas, in order to produce a reasonable crop.

Project Five

~

Clothing a wall with trellis

Bare walls have a nasty tendency to look bleak and ugly, but fortunately the use of trellis can effect an instant transformation. Not only does it provide a handsome plant support, but the design of the trellis itself creates plenty of visual interest too. The formal diamonds or squares of a trellis pattern stand out well against the plain background of a wall or fence, and such interest is especially useful where space is limited.

In this small courtyard garden the trellis has been used in an unusual fashion to create an illusion of space. Parts of the trellis have been angled out from the wall, so the eye sweeps in and out to follow its line and the garden appears larger as a result. The niches that have been formed by the angled trellis have been planted with ivy, which gives year-round interest with its glossy, evergreen leaves and needs virtually no maintenance into the bargain. The small diamond pattern of the dark brown trellis is shown up beautifully against the whitewashed walls, and the pale background also helps to create an impression of space and airiness.

~

Trellis is an ideal support for climbers against a wall, and these cleverly-angled pieces make the garden appear larger than it actually is.

MATERIALS

Trellis sufficient to cover the
required area

4–8 wooden spacers, 50 mm (2 in) square,
to each piece of trellis

Screws, length 10 cm (4 in). Allow
1 screw for each corner, plus 1 for each
mid-point where the panel is
1.2 m (4 ft) or longer

Galvanized metal right-angles and screws
(if making an angled trellis)

Equivalent number of wallplugs
as screws

Wood stain or preservative
(see page 19)

TOOLS

Electric drill with masonry drill bit of the
same diameter as the wallplugs, and
ordinary bit to drill clearance holes
for the screws

Saw, hammer

Screwdriver

Paint brush

Protective clothing

Using trellis with closely spaced battens
is a good idea in a tiny garden, as the
detailed pattern givens more interest from
the available space. However, this style
does tend to cost more than square-pat-
terned trellis with a wider spaced design.
In a bigger garden, there would be no bar
to using this cheaper trellis.

Types of trellis

Rigid wooden trellis comes in square or
diamond shapes. There is a number of different
variations with the patterns varying in size,
depending on the thickness or the quantity of
the wood used. There is a good range of
different panel sizes available too.

Expanding wooden trellis made of thin
pieces of wood can be pulled out lengthways
to the desired size – either long and thin or
short and wide – and screwed on to wooden
battens. Generally this type has a shorter life
than rigid trellis. Plastic-covered wire trellis
is really suitable only for small areas or for
single plants, as it tends to lack the strength
of wood.

Putting up trellis

Note. The trellis in the photograph on page
50 does not have wooden spacers at the top
because the top edge of the wall is slightly
protruding. It is advisable to have a gap
between wall and trellis to give plant stems
room to twine, and it also allows air to circulate
which helps prevent fungal diseases and rot.
Unless your wall is of similar design, use
wooden spacers to achieve the same effect.

If the trellis will be sitting directly on the
ground as in the photograph it's a good idea
to set the base on a 'sacrificial' piece of wood
to prevent the bottom edge of the trellis
becoming damp and rotting. All timber and
any cut edges are best treated with wood
preservative beforehand

1. The first panels to be put up are those that are set flat against the wall. With the trellis panels lying flat on the ground, drill a hole at each corner through the trellis and wooden spacer. Panels larger than 1.2 m (4 ft) benefit from being secured at the mid-points too (see Diagram 1).

2. Hold the trellis against the wall and mark on the wall the points that correspond to the drilled holes. On house walls, make sure that the lowest part of the trellis is above the damp-proof course. Then drill the holes in the wall and insert the wall plugs into them. Screw the trellis firmly on to the wall.

This is really a two-person job, as it's difficult to line up a piece of trellis single-handed.

3. To fix the angled sections of trellis together, use metal right-angles that already have holes for screws. Drill the trellis panels as before while they are flat on the ground and fix them together. Then stand them upright and screw them to the other panels that are already fixed to the wall.

Hinging trellis to its support

Putting up trellis with hinges can be very useful as you will probably need to gain access the wall or fence to carry out maintenance from time to time, such as painting the wall or treating the fence with wood

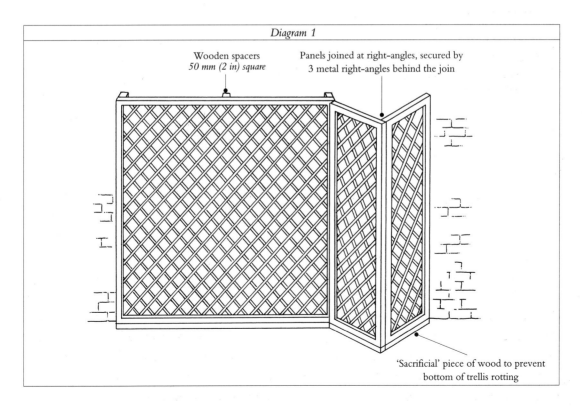

Diagram 1

Wooden spacers
50 mm (2 in) square

Panels joined at right-angles, secured by
3 metal right-angles behind the join

'Sacrificial' piece of wood to prevent
bottom of trellis rotting

Wall shrubs like Garrya elliptica *can be grown against trellis as well as a wall. In winter the bunches of dangling catkins provide welcome interest.*

~

preservative. This enables the panel of trellis, plants and all, to be unhooked at the top and lowered to the ground while the work is carried out.

Fix four wooden battens to the wall using the longest screws, to correspond to each corner of the trellis panel. Screw the other four battens on to the trellis panel. Fix the hinges to the underside of the lower pair of battens and the hooks and eyes to the top pair (see Diagram 2).

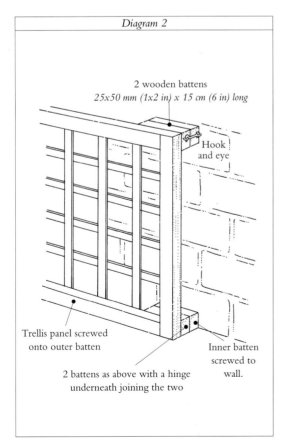

Diagram 2

2 wooden battens
25x50 mm (1x2 in) x 15 cm (6 in) long

Hook and eye

Trellis panel screwed onto outer batten

Inner batten screwed to wall.

2 battens as above with a hinge underneath joining the two

Fixing trellis on top of a wall or fence

Low walls and fences can be extended upwards by fixing trellis on top. In many cases this is desirable to create privacy from neighbours, or you may just wish to extend the growing area for your climbing plants. If the trellis will eventually support a reasonable amount of plant growth, do bear in mind that such growth will become weighty and will be subject to strong wind pressure, so it is important to fix the trellis very securely.

Provided the wall is in good condition and the site is sheltered from strong winds, the posts need extend only part-way down the wall, so long as they are secured with 15 cm (6 in) bolts or screws with wall plugs (see Diagram 3). However, should the strength of the wall or fence be at all in doubt, it's best to extend the uprights to the ground with the

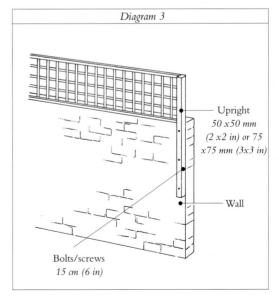

Diagram 3

Upright
50 x50 mm (2 x2 in) or 75 x75 mm (3x3 in)

Wall

Bolts/screws
15 cm (6 in)

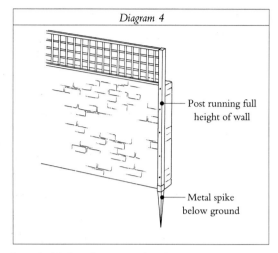

Diagram 4

Post running full
height of wall

Metal spike
below ground

base held firm by a metal spike (see Diagram 4). In a high wind the posts will take the weight of the plant-clad trellis rather than pressure being exerted on the wall itself. It may sound like unnecessary work, but it's worth remembering that people have been killed by walls crashing down during a gale.

Supporting plants with vine eyes and wires

If your aim is just to clothe a wall or fence with plants, the use of vine eyes – screws with a loop at the end – and strong wire, provides an inexpensive alternative to trellis. The wires are best spaced horizontally about 30 cm (12 in) apart with the lowest wire at the same distance from ground level. Vertical wires can be run between these horizontal ones, depending on the plant's habit. The vine eyes hold the wire a few centimetres away from the wall or fence, leaving room for the plant's stems to twine and for air to circulate around the foliage.

Plants for trellis

The vast majority of climbing plants are suitable for growing on trellis, as are wall shrubs that can be trained and tied in to their support. The most important point to consider is the aspect of the site – whether it is sunny or shady – because this tends to be very clearly defined with walls and fences (see page 9). Accordingly, the plants outlined below are divided according to their site preferences.

Part- or full shade (north- and east-facing sites)

Ivies are excellent for year-round interest, and there is a wealth of different varieties with prettily shaped or variegated leaves. It's best to avoid the most vigorous species, *Hedera colchica*, as it will eventually form a large mass of growth that will become very heavy. Instead, go for one of the *H. helix* varieties as these are the quickest to grow.

Those with attractively shaped leaves are best, such as *H. h.* 'Green Ripple' with jagged edged leaves. Alternatively there are many ivies with foliage that is variegated with gold or silver, such as the popular variety *H. h.* 'Goldheart' with leaves that have a bold central splash of yellow, or *H. h.* 'Glacier' that is grey-green and white.

Most clematis thrive in shade and indeed the large-flowered hybrids definitely prefer to have their roots in a cool spot. Though they are quite happy in the shade, the optimum position for hybrid clematis is to have their 'heads' in the sun. Clematis species however are equally happy in sun or shade.

To kick off the flowering season *Clematis alpina* and *C. macropetala* varieties are among the earliest to bloom. At the far end of the summer, species such as *Clematis viticella* bear flowers in many different colours, while *C. orientalis* and *C. tangutica* have beautiful golden 'lanterns' of flower.

Then, for summer fragrance, choose *Jasminum officinale* (summer jasmine) or one of the many honeysuckles. Also for summer blooms, clematis with pale, bi-coloured flowers such as 'Bee's Jubilee' and 'Nelly Moser' do especially well in shade as their blooms retain their colour well. Although most roses prefer sun, a few varieties do well in shade, including 'Danse de Feu' (red), 'Madame Alfred Carrière' (white flushed pink) and 'Maigold' (bronze-yellow). Good wall shrubs for shade include *Chaenomeles*, *Euonymus fortunei* cultivars, *Garrya elliptica*, *Jasminum nudiflorum* and *Pyracantha*.

Sun (south and west-facing sites)

For speedy growth, good climbers include *Passiflora caerulea* (passion flower) and *Humulus lupulus* 'Aureus' (Golden hop). In full sun, *Campsis* (trumpet flower) soon makes a wonderful display of attractive foliage and bright flowers. Clematis are ideal, though large-flowered hybrids benefit from having their roots shaded by tubs or ground-cover plants. Species clematis are less fussy, and a sheltered site would be suitable for evergreen clematis such as the charming, *C. cirrhosa*. Annual climbers such as *Cobaea scandens* and *Tropaeolum peregrinum* establish quickly for a colourful summer display.

In a really warm, sheltered spot, it would be worth trying some of the exotic plants that are on the border of hardiness. They include *Clianthus* (parrot's bill or lobster's claw) with its strangely shaped and bright flowers, or one of the frost-tender jasmines such as *J. mesnyi* (primrose jasmine) which bears large yellow delicately scented flowers. Some of the passion flowers with spectacular and ornate blooms may also survive outside in very mild areas.

Handsome wall shrubs include *Cytisus battandieri* that has pineapple-scented blooms, *Fremontodendron* with its magnificent golden-yellow saucers of flowers, *Piptanthus* which bears attractive, evergreen foliage and spikes of yellow flowers, and *Phygelius* which produces tall stems clad with tubular, brightly coloured blooms. One of the new, golden-leaved *Escallonias* could be pruned and trained against trellis where its leaves could make a lovely contrast to other flowers.

Roses make a superb display of summer flowers. Climbing varieties have a neater habit altogether than ramblers and this is particularly important if people are likely to be passing within close range of the thorny branches. Modern climbing roses may be the best choice for trellis as they are generally more compact than the old-fashioned ones. They also bear repeated flushes of flowers so they provide a longer period of colour in a high-profile position. To encourage the best show of flowers, train the branches horizontally or in a fan shape. This restricts the flow of sap which, in turn, stimulates flowering.

Project Six

~

Arches

An archway or a walk-through frame-work is the simplest of all the larger vertical features to construct, but one that can effect a transformation out of all proportion to its size. Apart from the obvious change of visual interest from the horizontal to the vertical, it is most valuable in making a transition from one area to another. Put an arch between two parts of the garden with different themes to accentuate the change in the two: from the patio into the main part of the garden, for example, or from a flower-bordered lawn into the vegetable garden.

Elsewhere in the garden an arch over a pathway makes it more enticing to walk down and if you put two or more arches along the path they will create a false sense of perspective, making the path seem longer than it actually is. Emphasize an entrance by combining an arch with a gateway, and give it an extra-special touch by clothing it with fragrant climbers – imagine being welcomed home by the sweet scent of jasmine, honey-suckle or roses. Yet another option is to use this feature in a static form and create a pleasant plant-clad bower, by placing it over a seat that has its back against a fence or hedge. All in all, an archway can be adapted for just about anywhere in the garden.

Ready-made arches are widely available in a range of designs and materials. The cheapest

---

MATERIALS

4 fence posts 75 mm (3 in) square and 2.1 m (7 ft) high

Metal spikes or concrete in which to set the posts (see page 26 for options)

2 pieces of rigid trellis, 45 cm x 1.8 m (18 in x 6 ft)

Timber 50 x 75 mm (2 x 3 in) for the over-head framework in the following lengths; 2 pieces 1.2 m (4 ft) long; 2 pieces 45 cm (18 in) long

2 pieces of timber 50 mm (2 in) square and 1.5 m (5 ft) long for the crossbraces, to be cut into pieces 45 cm (18 in) long

Galvanized nails: 24 nails 50 mm (2 in) long; approx. 8 nails 75 mm (3 in) long; 24 nails 10 cm (4 in) long

Wood stain or preservative (see page 19)

---

ones are made of plastic-covered wire or thin wood, but they tend to last for only a relatively short while. It's worth spending a little more money and buying a reasonably robust arch made of stout trellis, timber or

~

An archway makes a lovely plant-clad 'doorway' to accentuate the transition from one part of the garden to another.

TOOLS

Electric drill with bits a little smaller in diameter than the longest and shortest nails

Paint brush

Protective clothing

Tape measure and measuring lines

Spirit level

Saw

Hammer

Stepladder

wrought iron, the choice of which is obviously dependent on your taste and budget. Now the old country crafts are making a comeback it's even possible to buy beautifully constructed arches made of woven willow or hazel. You need not be limited to your local source of supply either as most arches can be despatched by carriers at a reasonable cost.

However, an arch or framework is straightforward to construct, particularly if it is made to a simple design like the one in the photograph on page 59. This flat-topped framework is built using fence posts braced with crosspieces, joined at the top by smaller pieces of timber and filled in with trellis at the sides. Clad with two clematis and a climbing rose, it makes a pretty feature and a definite transition from the shady, woodland-style part of the garden to a lighter and more open area. The items listed on the previous page are sufficient for an arch measuring 2.1 m (7 ft) high and 1.2 m (4 ft) wide.

Constructing the arch

1. Using a tape measure and measuring lines mark out the sites for the posts and put them up (see page 26), leaving a gap of approximately 45 cm (18 in) between each pair of posts. It's best to use the trellis as a marker for measuring this gap as the size of the trellis panels may vary a little.

2. Cut the timber for the framework and crossbraces to match the gaps between the posts. Paint the cut ends with wood preservative and let it dry. Using 7.5 cm (3 in) nails, nail the overhead framework of 50 x 75 mm (2 x 3 in) wood on top of the posts with the longer side flat against the tops of the posts (see diagram below).

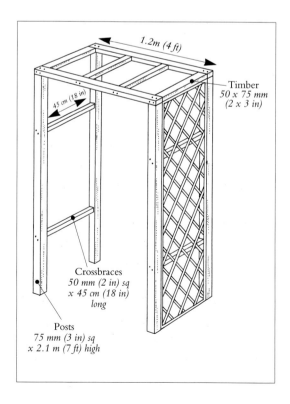

1.2m (4 ft)

45 cm (18 in)

Timber
50 x 75 mm
(2 x 3 in)

Crossbraces
50 mm (2 in) sq
x 45 cm (18 in)
long

Posts
75 mm (3 in) sq
x 2.1 m (7 ft) high

3. Prepare to nail the crosspieces into place, using the longest nails. The nails will need to go through the post first, so the points go into the end of each crosspiece. Rather than just hammering in the nails, the force of which may well knock the posts out of alignment, it's best to drill holes for them first. Use a drill bit that is slightly smaller than the width of the nail. Once one end of each crosspiece has been nailed into place, use the spirit level to check that it is level before securing the other end.

4. Finally nail the trellis on to the sides of the framework using the shortest nails. As before, drill holes for the nails first. The trellis should sit between the posts and rest against the crosspieces. Finish off by giving the whole structure a coat of wood stain or preservative so that all the timber is the same colour.

How to make a rustic framework

For an informal part of the garden, a framework made of round, rustic poles is an attractive feature that is cheap and quick to construct. The design can be based on the framework in the diagram to the left, with the main variation being that all the timber is the same size. The post ends are sunk into the ground, preferably in concrete so that they last longer, and therefore you'll need to allow an extra 45–60 cm (18–24 in) length on each upright post. The framework can simply be nailed together using 10-cm (4-in) nails. Any protruding nail ends should be hammered flat to avoid danger of injury.

Plants for the arch

Climbers for an archway need to have enough growth to make the arch look well dressed but not smother it with foliage so that it becomes unbalanced and top-heavy.

Some of the best plants are herbaceous ones as they die back to ground level in winter yet regrow rapidly in spring. They include *Lathyrus* species (perennial sweet peas) and *Eccremocarpus scaber* (Chilean glory flower) for a site in full sun, and *Humulus lupulus* 'Aureus' (golden hop) for sun or partial shade. There are several climbers that don't mind being hacked back almost to ground level every year or two if they have formed an over-abundant mass of growth. They include *Passiflora caerulea* (passion flower), and the clematis species *C. orientalis*, *C. tangutica*, *C. texensis* and *C. viticella*.

Roses look wonderful on archways, but it is usually best to go for climbers of compact habit, rather than those exuberant ramblers that fling out thorny branches to catch the unwary passer-by. Look for longer-flowering varieties like 'Aloha', 'Breath of Life', 'Dreamgirl' or 'Schoolgirl', and the miniature climbers 'Laura Ford' and 'Warm Welcome'. The large-flowered clematis hybrids make excellent partners for roses.

Add a touch of winter colour with *Jasminum nudiflorum* (winter jasmine), which can easily be grown up a pillar provided the shoots are tied in occasionally. Remember to prune it each year immediately after flowering to keep its growth neat and tidy.

Project Seven

~

Free-standing supports for climbers

Out in the garden borders the versatility of climbing plants can really be given full rein. A border looks so much better right through the year if the plants are growing at a variety of levels, and with the help of climbers there's no need to wait for years while trees and shrubs reach a decent size. Free-standing supports for climbers can easily be incorporated into a border to transform it with some instant height, creating spectacular columns of flowers and foliage that flourish above a tapestry of lower-growing shrubs and perennials. Away from the borders such supports can be used as stand-alone features around the garden: as a single specimen in a lawn, for example, or as a focal point to draw the eye at the end of a pathway or pergola. Make the most of your natural climbing plant supports too – that is, well-established trees and shrubs that can be given an extra burst of colour by having climbers trained through them. In addition any immovable objects such as tree stumps or telegraph poles can be turned from eyesores into handsome features with the aid of climbing plants.

~

A frame for climbing plants can easily be constructed in a border to give it some instant height. This triangular framework is made of rustic wooden poles, and it can be put together very quickly.

Ready-made supports are available in a wide selection of styles and materials to suit just about every taste and budget. Ironwork obelisks look superb, either used singly or, if your budget allows you to splash out, in a group of three, of varying heights for extra interest.

Wrought iron is very handsome, and plastic-coated tubular steel is similar in appearance. Both materials are long-lasting and low-maintenance, though wrought iron will need occasional treatment with special paint to prevent corrosion. The height of these obelisks is around 1.5–2.4 m (5–8 ft).

Plant supports made of woven willow twigs and hazel poles are becoming increasingly popular. The free-standing ones are lovely, conical frames with hazel poles forming a wigwam shape and held together with several bands of beautifully woven willow. Heights range from around 1.2–1.8 m (4–6 ft) and, given the work involved, the prices are often surprisingly reasonable.

At the top end of the price range are obelisks made of galvanized wirework and craftsman-made wooden ones, constructed to beautiful and extremely decorative designs. However, these superbly crafted features are probably more accurately described as garden ornaments than plant supports, as they need just the lightest dressing of foliage to emphasize their elegant lines.

All the supports described above can be put up simply by pushing the legs a few centimetres into the soil. However, in some cases it is better to have a firmer foundation: in an exposed, windy site, for example, or if the structure will be supporting a lot of plant growth. Extra security can be given by driving metal pegs or short wooden posts into the ground first, then wiring the legs of the support discreetly on to them.

In addition to all these ready-made structures on the market there is plenty of potential for making your own climbing-plant supports and, even better, they don't need to be large or complex in order to be effective.

On the simplest level, a 1.8–2.4 m (6–8 ft) fence post can be driven into the ground and wrapped round with a cylinder of plastic or wire mesh. Though utilitarian in appearance, this basic structure will rapidly disappear under the fast-growing shoots of clematis, for instance, or the scrambling stems of *Eccremocarpus*. A basic wigwam of 1.8 m (6 ft) bamboo canes can support a lightweight planting of annuals such as *Lathyrus* (sweet peas) or *Ipomoea* (morning glory), while one made of stout rustic poles, nailed at the top or tied using strong wire, could host a considerably larger plant such as a rambler rose.

Of course, the benefits of these simple supports are that they can be put up quickly and cost next to nothing, so they're particularly useful for creating an interesting structure in a new garden without breaking the bank.

Other home-made free-standing supports range from simple features that take very little time and money to construct, to those which require slightly more time and some basic carpentry skills.

Rustic frame

A three-cornered frame of the type featured in the photograph on the previous page is perfect for supporting roses. The stems of climbing or rambler roses can be wound around the outside of the frame so that they gradually spiral upwards, with the added bonus that bending the stems in this fashion restricts the flow of sap which will help promote flowering. Such a frame could also be constructed on a larger scale to contain the sprawling growth of the larger old shrub roses like the more vigorous hybrids of *Rosa gallica* and *R. rugosa*, which are lovely but unruly plants for the back of the border.

To make the frame take three rustic fence posts of between 1.8 and 2.4 m (6 and 8 ft) long and hammer them into the ground to form a triangle (see diagram, right). The spacing between each post can vary from 45 to 75 cm (18 to 30 in), depending on the size of frame you wish to make and the vigour of the plants that it is intended to support. Between each pair of posts, nail three crossbraces of the same wood. Although the flat ends of the bracing pieces can simply be nailed on to each post, you can make a smoother finish if desired by shaping the ends of the braces so that they fit between the uprights.

Unless you buy rustic fence posts which have already been treated with wood preservative, it is a good idea to give the poles at least two coats of preservative before putting the frame together. The parts of the posts that will be below ground need special attention: soak these ends in wood preservative for 24 hours and leave to dry for a similar length of time.

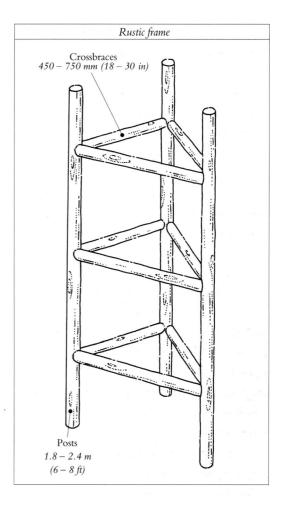

Rustic frame

Crossbraces
450 – 750 mm (18 – 30 in)

Posts
*1.8 – 2.4 m
(6 – 8 ft)*

Rope swags

Make a stylish back-of-the-border feature with swags of sturdy rope hung between wooden pillars. The pillars take the bulk of the plants' weight, while a few stems can be trained out to drape elegantly along the ropes, garlanding them with flowers.

To make each pillar use four posts 50 mm (2 in) square and 2.1 m (7 ft) long and join them with pieces of 25 x 50 mm (1 x 2 in) wood. These crosspieces are 10 cm (4 in)

long and spaced 30 cm (12 in) apart (see diagram below). So for a pillar that would stand 1.8 m (6 ft) from ground level, you will need a total of 2.4 m (8 ft) of wood for the crosspieces and 24 nails 7.5 cm (3 in) long with which to secure them. Space the pillars a minimum of 2.4 m (8 ft) apart.

Once the pillars are complete, put them up by setting the base in concrete (see page 26) with the bottom 30 cm (12 in) of each one below ground level. When all the pillars are up, run the ropes through their centres and secure each loose end of rope with nails.

A similar but simpler alternative is to use fence posts on their own, with thin rope that is held in place by large, galvanized staples hammered into the post.

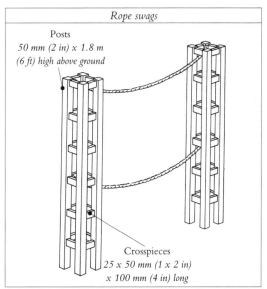

Rope swags

Posts
50 mm (2 in) x 1.8 m
(6 ft) high above ground

Crosspieces
25 x 50 mm (1 x 2 in)
x 100 mm (4 in) long

*Stout ropes can be run between posts
or pillars to create elegant,
flower-dressed swags.*

Bicycle-wheel 'Maypole'

All sorts of throwaway items can be adapted for use in the garden. One such item is the rim of an old bicycle wheel which can form a maypole-shaped frame (see diagram below).

The wheel rim is laid out flat on the ground, held down by long pieces of galvanized wire bent into 'hairpins' and buried in the ground. A 2.1 m (7 ft) bamboo cane is pushed into the ground in the centre, the top of which is first notched in the shape of a cross using a hacksaw. Strong string or wire can then be run through the old spoke holes in the wheel and over the top of the cane, sitting securely in the notches on the top. Five to seven strings give the best effect. This support is ideal for lightweight plants such as annuals, a compact clematis, runner beans or herbaceous climbers. During the winter

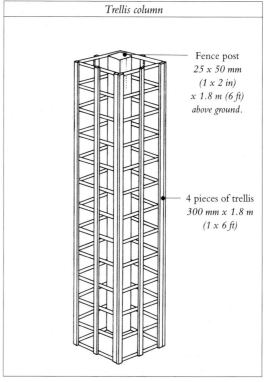

Trellis column

Fence post
*25 x 50 mm
(1 x 2 in)
x 1.8 m (6 ft)
above ground.*

4 pieces of trellis
*300 mm x 1.8 m
(1 x 6 ft)*

months, this support does not look very attractive, but it can be easily dismantled and re-erected in the spring.

Trellis column or pyramid

Take four pieces of 30 cm x 1.8 m (1 x 6 ft) trellis and nail them together to form a column (see diagram). To put it up, hammer a 2.1-m (7-ft) fence post – one that is 50 mm (2 in) square would be adequate – into the ground and slide the trellis column over it.

The post should sit in one corner of the column and the trellis can be screwed or nailed on to it. In a similar vein, four pieces of fan-shaped trellis can be wired together to form a pyramid-shape.

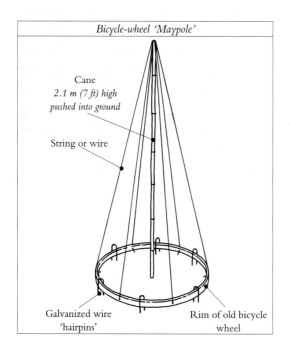

Bicycle-wheel 'Maypole'

Cane
*2.1 m (7 ft) high
pushed into ground*

String or wire

Galvanized wire
'hairpins'

Rim of old bicycle
wheel

68

Plants for free-standing supports

Compact plants for small supports

Slender, lightweight plants are necessary for smaller, free-standing supports, which could otherwise be brought to the ground by the sheer weight of foliage. Most, but not all annual climbers are excellent: my favourites for this purpose include *Ipomoea* (morning glory) which needs a sunny and sheltered spot in order to produce its exquisite blue flowers; the annual *Lathyrus* species, including the ever-popular sweet peas; and *Rhodochiton atrosanguineus* (purple bell vine) with its unusual, purple-black flowers.

Clematis viticella varieties are ideal because they are best cut back almost to ground level in early spring, so they don't build up a tan-gled mass of growth. Varieties range in colour from white to pale mauve, deep purple to bright red. *C. texensis* varieties do best in a sheltered spot, where they produce their bell-shaped blooms in late summer.

Plants for larger supports

Annual climbers with a more vigorous habit are excellent for obelisks and tripods. *Tropaeolum peregrinum* (canary creeper) is a hardy annual that is very easy to grow, quickly flinging up long stems covered in yellow, fringed flowers. Indeed, it can even become a bit of a pest if it is allowed to self-seed, though I'm more than happy with such behaviour as any unwanted seedlings can easily be pulled up. The popular nasturtium (*Tropaeolum majus*) is an easily grown plant to create a pillar of vibrant colour. In need of a little nurturing is *Cobaea scandens* (cup-and-saucer plant), which is best started off under cover in late winter. It needs a long season of growth in order to produce its unusual purple or white blooms.

Most clematis make a lovely display on larger supports, and the vast majority of species and hybrids are suitable for such sites. The main exceptions are the evergreens, which need their backs against a warm wall, and *C. montana*, which is extremely vigorous.

Roses are perfect for swags and frameworks. Of the old-fashioned types, ramblers are better than climbers because most of their old growth is pruned out each year after flowering. Modern climbers, however, are useful for pillars and obelisks as they are generally compact in habit, growing to around 2.4–3 m (8–10 ft). Several newer miniature climbers grow to only about 1.8 m (6 ft) high; they include 'Laura Ford' (yellow) and 'Warm Welcome' (orange).

Project Eight

~

A half-pergola

A substantial half-pergola is perfect for adding height to a garden boundary or sectioning off a part of the garden, like this patio and seating area. As it lacks the enclosing overhead beams of a full pergola, it lends an attractive air of seclusion to the patio without losing any feeling of space. In areas subject to high rainfall it is also better to do away with overhead beams to avoid the constant dripping of rainwater.

The fence and seat in the picture have been stained to match the pergola to give a feeling of overall harmony, though this pergola would look equally good as a stand-alone feature. The beauty of the design is that it can be easily adapted to the needs of a particular site, though this style of pergola does tend to look best in a reasonably modern setting. Here it curves gently round the seat, which is done by shaping the ends of the joining beams at an angle. If you don't want to bother with the shaping, it is much quicker and easier to build the pergola in a straight line.

Reasonable carpentry skills are required for building this pergola. To make construction

~

A half-pergola makes an attractive feature,
and its clean-cut lines are particularly in keeping
with a modern garden.

MATERIALS

6 posts 100 mm (4 in) square to stand a minimum of 1.8 m (6 ft) above ground

Metal spikes or concrete in which to set the posts (see page 26 for options)

Timber 50 x 100 mm (2 x 4 in) in the following lengths:

5 crosspieces 60 cm (2 ft) long to run between the posts

6 overhead beams 90 cm (3 ft) long

6 diagonal braces 60 cm (2 ft) long

30 screws, length 75 mm (3 in)

20 wooden dowels, length 75 mm (3 in), and wood adhesive

Wood stain or preservative (see page 19)

TOOLS

Set square and pencil

Electric drill with bits of the same diameter as the screws and dowels

Spirit level

Saw, hammer, chisel

File, screwdriver

Stepladder

more straightforward, the size of the beams and crosspieces have been slightly reduced compared to the size of those in the photograph. However, if you wanted to build a structure using timbers that all measured 100 x 100 mm (4 x 4 in), it would be necessary to have good carpentry skills in order to joint the

pieces of wood. For example, the post and overhead beam would be best joined with a mortise-and-tenon joint.

A similar design of pergola is available in kit form. It comprises rafters that are notched to sit on a single overhead beam that joins the posts, though it lacks the diagonal crosspieces of the pergola shown here.

The items listed to the left are sufficient for a pergola measuring 3 m (10 ft) long.

Constructing the half-pergola

1. Before putting up the supporting posts, it's essential to put together the overhead beam and bracing piece of each one (see diagram, right). Cut notches in the tops of the posts by making several vertical cuts with the saw and chiselling the pieces out at the bottom. If necessary, sand or file the base so that it is smooth. The notch should be 5 cm (2 in) wide and 7.5 cm (3 in) deep. Treat the cut surfaces with wood preservative and allow it to dry. (Do the same for any other cut surfaces, below.) Alternatively you could save a bit of work and buy posts that are already notched.

2. The overhead beam also needs to be notched to take the crosspiece. Cut a notch 5 cm (2 in) wide and high and 2.5 cm (1 in) deep. This notch should be situated on the part of the beam that will be just forward of the top of the posts. If the pergola is to be curved as in the photograph, these notches and the ends of the crosspiece need to be cut at an angle. Prepare the crosspieces at the same time to sit in the notches on the overhead

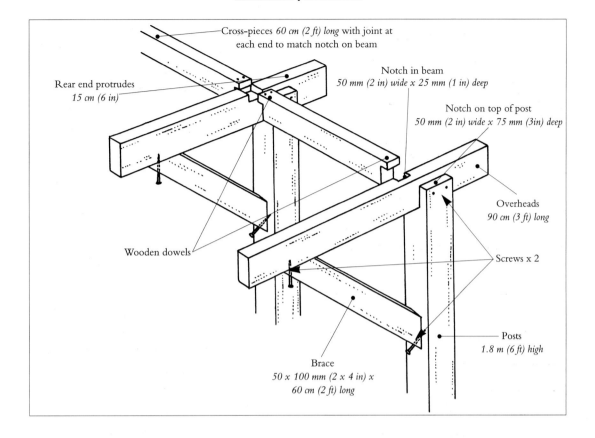

Cross-pieces *60 cm (2 ft) long* with joint at
each end to match notch on beam

Notch in beam
50 mm (2 in) wide x 25 mm (1 in) deep

Rear end protrudes
15 cm (6 in)

Notch on top of post
50 mm (2 in) wide x 75 mm (3in) deep

Overheads
90 cm (3 ft) long

Wooden dowels

Screws x 2

Posts
1.8 m (6 ft) high

Brace
*50 x 100 mm (2 x 4 in) x
60 cm (2 ft) long*

beams, by cutting out a piece of wood 5 cm (2 in) square from the underside at each end. Drill holes for the wooden dowels – two in each joint – to run vertically through both the crosspieces and the overhead beams.

3. Set the overhead beam in the notch on top of the post, with the end protruding 15 cm (6 in) beyond the post to the rear. Drill two holes for the screws to run horizontally through the notch on top of each post and into the beam. Fix the screws in place.

4. For the bracing piece, cut the ends at an angle so it fits snugly against the post and overhead beam. Cut a shallow notch in the post for the lower end of the bracing piece. Once the angles of this piece have been cut

to your satisfaction and before it is fixed in place, it's a good idea to cut and shape the other bracing pieces at the same time, using the first piece as a guide. Drill holes for the screws, going upwards at an angle of approximately 45 degrees into the post and overhead beam, and fix them in place.

5. Once each upright section has been fixed together as above, put up the posts. To get the spacing right, it's advisable to put up the first one and then use the crosspiece as a marker for the next, and so on. Use the spirit level to make sure that all the posts are exactly upright, and if you are making a curving pergola, take care that all the posts are set at complementary angles.

6. The uprights can now be joined together with the crosspieces. Sit them in the prepared notches, securing them with the wooden dowels. Apply wood adhesive to the dowels before fixing them in place.

Plants for the pergola

This design of pergola benefits from planting that is bold yet restrained, to allow the clean lines of the structure to show clearly. In the photograph on page 70 the ornamental vine *Vitis coignetiae* spreads its long, trailing stems over the beams to clothe them with its large, handsome leaves. Each lobed leaf can be up to 30 cm (12 in) across, and in autumn the foliage turns from green to glowing shades of crimson and scarlet, giving a magnificent display. The autumn colour is best where the soil is not very fertile, or where the roots are restricted, and this plant is not fussy about growing either in sun or shade.

Another striking plant for sun or shade is *Parthenocissus henryana*. Its large, lobed leaves are dark green with veins prominently traced in silver. This plant also has good autumn colour, though not as dramatic as that of the ornamental vine described above.

Other plants with bold foliage include *Wisteria,* with its large, pinnate leaves and long racemes of fragrant flowers in late spring. *Campsis* (trumpet vine) also has pinnate leaves, and in summer it bears beautiful and exotic trumpet-shaped flowers, which are bright red or yellow in colour. *Actinidia kolomikta* has heart-shaped green leaves that are prominently tipped with cream and pink. All these plants need a reasonably sunny and sheltered site.

One of the large-leaved ivies (*Hedera colchica* spp.) would be ideal for some evergreen foliage interest. A variegated form such as *H.c.* 'Dentata Variegata' would stand out particularly well; its adult leaves become slightly elongated, giving the whole plant an appearance of gracefully draping itself over its support.

How to attach plants to posts

When plants are to be grown up the posts of any structure, it is necessary to give them some form of extra support, even with self-clinging plants such as ivy and Virginia creeper as the post or pillar rarely has enough rough surfaces for the plant to grip on. There are several ways to do this. Pieces of wire or plastic mesh can be wrapped around each post and secured with U-shaped metal staples – galvanized ones are best as they won't rust.

Remember to leave a little space – about 2.5 cm (1 inch) or so – between the mesh and the post so the plant has room to twine. Another option is to hammer nails into the post and run wires between them. Thirdly, you can tie in the plant's stems as they grow, but this will need doing weekly during the growing season.

~

Solanum jasminoides 'Album' with its ice-white flowers is a lovely climber for a sunny pergola or an archway. However, it does need a reasonably sheltered spot as it can be susceptible to frost damage in a severe winter.

~

Climbers in containers

Although in the past climbers have been used mainly in borders, there is absolutely no bar to using them in containers. In recent years the dwindling size of modern plots and town gardens, along with a growing interest in furnishing the patio with plants, has created a considerable amount of interest in this direction. With a good range of pots and supports now available, it's not unusual these days to see a tall pillar of pretty flowers or attractive foliage making a marvellous centrepiece to a display of containers. On a practical level such climbers can often be used to create privacy around a patio or seating area too.

Many different materials can be used to support container-grown climbers. Simplest and cheapest of the home-made options are ordinary bamboo canes, which can be placed in a container to form a tripod or pyramid shape. Alternatively use garden raffia to tie the canes together in a fan or trellis shape to create an attractive and oriental effect. If you can get hold of any willow prunings, they can be woven together to make an unusual and stylish support as shown in the photograph on page 79.

Lovers of topiary who don't wish to spend a fair few years growing and training box (*Buxus sempervirens*) into intricate shapes — or spending a small fortune on ready-grown specimens – can turn to wire topiary frames. They come in a range of shapes including spirals, pyramids and 'lollipops'. Just plant several small-leaved ivies (*Hedera helix* cultivars) in a pot, set up your frame and train the ivy over it. In a couple of years you'll have an exceptionally handsome specimen. It can be a good idea to grow these topiaries in pairs, to flank a doorway or a flight of steps, for example.

Ready-made supports tend to vary enormously in style and price. Trellis panels are most economical: buy them either as long, narrow panels, such as the one measuring 30 cm x 1.8 m (1 x 6 ft) in the photograph on page 78, or in fan shapes. Such trellis can be fixed either to stakes in a pot for a free-standing display, or direct to a wall or fence. Obelisks made of wood, nylon-clad steel tubing, decorative wire and wrought iron are all readily available.

A considerable range of climbing plants can be grown in pots, though it's important to take a bit of time and trouble over their cultural conditions to be sure of a good display. First choose a container that is large enough, which usually means a half-barrel or something similar, to house one or two permanent plants. As a general guide, it should be a minimum of 30 cm (12 in) wide and 38 cm (15 in) deep. It is vital that drainage is good or water will build up in winter when it can freeze and damage the roots. Ensure that the container has plenty of drainage holes, put a layer of crocks, stones or chunks of broken polystyrene in the base and raise the container a few centimetres off the ground so that water can easily drain away (see the diagram below).

For planting always use a good compost: a soil-based one such as John Innes no. 3 is ideal as the loam provides more of a buffer against drought than soilless composts. Don't be tempted to economize and use garden soil, which is rarely suitable. Remember that if you want the plant to perform well for quite a number of years, it needs to have its roots in some really good compost.

However, the key to success is not just in the planting. Regular maintenance in the form of feeding and watering is essential as the plant will depend on you to provide all its needs. It is rare indeed for rain to supply enough water, particularly if the container stands in the shelter of a wall. Depending on the site and the size of both the pot and the plant, it may need watering as often as once or twice a day in hot weather. Even in autumn and winter, don't overlook the need for a little water occasionally if the weather is dry for long periods. Should your schedule make regular watering a problem, it's worth considering one of the automatic watering systems with a timer that are now available for the ordinary gardener. Such a system really comes into its own at holiday times.

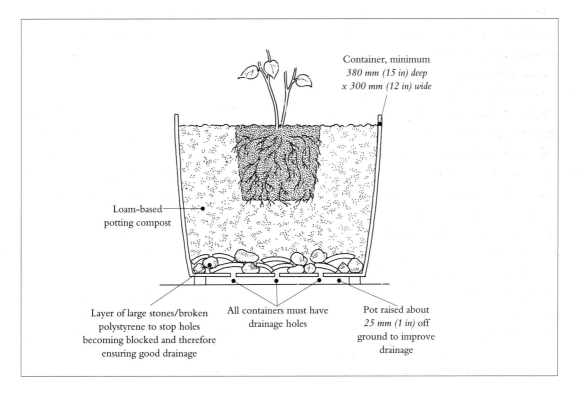

Container, minimum
380 mm (15 in) deep
x 300 mm (12 in) wide

Loam-based potting compost

Layer of large stones/broken polystyrene to stop holes becoming blocked and therefore ensuring good drainage

All containers must have drainage holes

Pot raised about *25 mm (1 in)* off ground to improve drainage

When it comes to feeding, which is necessary during the main growing period of early spring to late summer, there are two main options from which to choose. Add a liquid fertilizer to the water every week during the growing season, or apply some controlled-release fertilizer granules in the spring and top up with a few liquid feeds in summer when the granules start to become exhausted. Top-dressing, which is scraping off the top few centimetres of old compost in spring and replacing it with fresh potting compost, will also give the plant a boost.

In winter, the roots of climbers in containers can be susceptible to frost damage as all of the rootball is above ground. Efficient drainage goes a long way towards ensuring your plants' safety, as a sodden rootball can freeze solid and the roots can be badly damaged.

Should severe frosts threaten, it's a good idea to provide some extra protection. If the pots are moveable, put them closer together and against a wall, or even in an unheated greenhouse, porch or conservatory. Insulate outdoor pots by wrapping them with bubble polythene, ordinary polythene or sacking stuffed with straw. If conditions are forecast to become really bad, cover the plant itself with polythene or horticultural fleece. You must take off the covering as soon as the weather improves or it will provide ideal conditions for fungal diseases to flourish and all your good work could go to waste.

~

Above: A piece of trellis can be placed in a large container to make an instant support for climbers, in this case a honeysuckle.

~

Right: Willow twigs are very flexible and they can be woven together to make a charming support, in this case for some sweet peas.

Plants for containers

Although most climbers can be grown in pots, it's best to opt for those which are relatively compact in habit as vigorous ones can soon shoot up to leave a mass of unattractive, bare stems at the base. In a high-profile position – by a doorway, for example – choose plants that look good for a long period of time, such as those with evergreen or colourful foliage, or long-lasting flowers. If you have a greenhouse or conservatory, there is potential for growing frost-tender climbers as they can be moved under cover for the duration of winter.

Large flowered hybrid clematis are excellent for containers, though they do best when the pot is shaded as they dislike having hot roots. Several ways of doing this are to place the pot where it gets sun for only part of the day, plant smaller trailing plants around the edge such as ivy and creeping Jenny (*Lysimachia nummularia*), or put a cluster of small pots around the larger one that holds the clematis. Some hybrids perform better than others in containers. Good varieties which are free-flowering yet with a compact habit include 'Arctic Queen' (white), 'Asao' (deep pink), 'Daniel Deronda' (deep purple), 'Fireworks' (blue, red stripe), 'Pink Champagne' (cerise), 'Silver Moon' (pale mauve) and 'Sunset' (red, purple edge). The less vigorous clematis species such as *C. alpina C. viticella* and *C. macropetala* can also be grown in containers.

A fan of trellis or bamboo canes is an ideal support for wall shrubs such as abutilons with their showy, bell-shaped flowers, *Euonymus fortunei* varieties with attractively variegated foliage, and *Aloysia triphylla* (lemon verbena), which has leaves that give off a delicious lemon scent when bruised. All but the *Euonymus* need to over-winter under cover in all but the mildest areas, as will frost-tender plants such as *Tweedia* and *Sollya*, both of which have beautiful blue flowers.

Climbers with variegated foliage look good on fans or upright supports. Small-leaved ivies (*Hedera helix*) are evergreen and come in a wide range of different leaf colours, from green-and-grey varieties such as 'Glacier', 'Goldheart' with dark green leaves that have a central splash of gold, and 'Buttercup' that is completely yellow. Deciduous climbers include gold and variegated forms of *Jasminum officinale* and *Ampelopsis brevipendunculata* 'Elegans' with unusual pink-, white-and-green leaves.

Herbaceous climbers do well in containers where they make a handsome summer display. The best ones are *Eccremocarpus scaber* (Chilean glory flower), which will quickly scramble up a support of mesh or netting to produce its clusters of brightly coloured flowers over a long period, and *Humulus lupulus* 'Aureus' (golden hop) which has thin stems that can be wound over and around its support as the plant grows to produce a column of beautiful golden foliage. Once the plant dies down in the autumn, the dead stems can be cut back to soil level and the pot can be placed in a sheltered, out-of-the-way corner for the winter until it comes into growth again in the spring.

Roses were generally unsuitable for containers until recently, because of their deep and spreading root systems. However, over the past few years, several miniature climbers have been introduced which can be grown in large containers such as wooden half-barrels. They are 'Laura Ford' (yellow), 'Little Rambler' (blush pink), 'Nice Day' (salmon pink), 'Rosalie Coral' (orange-yellow) and 'Warm Welcome' (orange). Given the everlasting popularity of roses, they are sure to be joined by other varieties before too long.

Many vegetables are ideal candidates for pots, which can be very useful when there is little space for vegetables in the borders of today's small gardens. Climbing vegetables can be extremely ornamental too. There are runner beans, which produce clusters of red, white or bi-coloured flowers over a long period followed by masses of delicious beans.

Don't forget the marrows and squashes too; the fruits of some of the squashes in particular can be really ornamental and they make a real talking point. However, in order to produce a reasonable crop from all these vegetables, it is necessary to have a container that is about 45–60 cm (18–24 in) deep, so there is enough compost for these deep-rooting and hungry plants. It is important to feed them on a regular basis too, either with a weekly application of liquid fertilizer or by adding controlled-release fertilizer to the compost at planting time and topping up with a few liquid feeds in later summer.

Types of containers

There is an enormous selection of containers on the market today, in lots of different materials. For permanent plants, it's best to choose a material such as wood, terracotta or stone, as they provide reasonable insulation in the winter and also prevent the roots from becoming too hot in summer. When it comes to size, the larger the better is the rule for permanent plants, as a reasonable amount of root space gives a better environment for the plant as well as making the job of repotting much less frequent into the bargain. It is vital that all containers have adequate drainage holes, too. Where a plant may need potting-on in future, choose a container with a flared top so that the plant can be tipped out easily rather than an urn-shape from which it is almost impossible to extract the rootball without causing damage.

Wooden containers that are sufficiently large are usually half-barrels or tailor-made tubs. If you're buying a wooden half-barrel that has been previously used for storing something else, take care to first check that it hasn't contained a toxic material such as oil, and make sure that the metal hoops surrounding the barrel are in good condition.

Terracotta and glazed pots come in an enormous range of shapes and decorative finishes. Where the container is intended for year-round use outside, it is well worth spending a little extra on a pot which is guaranteed to be frostproof. Before planting up a terracotta or stone pot, give it a good soaking in water for several hours or the pot will 'rob' the compost of water to begin with.

Project Ten

~

Trompe l'oeil
features

The phrase *trompe l'oeil* literally translates from the French as 'something that deceives the eye', and in the garden it refers to features that create a sense of illusion and give the impression that the available space is larger than it is in reality. Although such features have been employed over the centuries in gardens of all sizes, they are most useful in small gardens or courtyards where space is severely limited.

The easiest way to achieve this illusion of space is to use a piece of artfully designed trellis with wooden battens that all point towards a single vanishing point in the centre, and which therefore give the impression of 'pushing back' the wall on which it sits. Although it is possible to make your own trellis, it is a time-consuming and skilful job and it would be better to opt for one of the many different ready-made reasonably priced designs that are available.

A piece of *trompe l'oeil* trellis really needs a bit of window-dressing in order to give the full benefit of the illusion. Start with the piece of bare wall in the centre and paint it a different colour from the surrounding brick-work. Then plant one or two climbing plants and carefully train them around the outer edges of the trellis to blend it in with its surround. Finally place an ornamental pot or a piece of sculpture in front of it to emphasize the feature further.

The site for the trellis should be carefully chosen for maximum effect. It really needs to be placed at a focal point – that is, the view-point at the end of a pathway or at one end of a courtyard – so that it draws the eye and becomes the centre of attention.

There are several ways in which to increase the deception. Mirrors can be of enormous benefit in tiny gardens, just as in the house, by reflecting light and appearing to double the available space. A full-length mirror surrounded by a trellis arch on which climbing plants are trained can make an incredible difference to a small space. If the mirror is set at a very slight angle, any person approaching it will not see their own reflection and so it further heightens the illusion. A good place to site a mirror is at

~

Pieces of trompe l'oeil *trellis can be bought ready-made. By creating a false sense of perspective, it gives an impression of space – very welcome in this small courtyard garden.*

the end of a pathway or a strip of lawn, as it then looks as though the paving or grass in the garden actually continues for a long way. If grass is used, keep it well trimmed where it meets the base of the mirror or it will spoil the impression.

If you are artistically inclined, a well painted mural can make a superb feature within a trellis or brick arch. If can be designed to give a three-dimensional, you can transform a tiny garden.

Plants for the *trompe l'oeil* feature

The decorative qualities of the trellis must not be obscured, so only the outer portion should be covered by whatever plants you choose. For this purpose opt for plants with a compact habit, ideally ones that will give colour for a long period of time. The large-flowered *Clematis* 'Nelly Moser' in the photograph is perhaps a little too vigorous; varieties that are more compact include 'Asao' (carmine-pink with a paler bar), 'Dawn' (palest pink) and 'Elsa Spath' (violet-blue).

Plants with attractive foliage are less showy but give a longer period of interest. Good ones for sun include forms of Jasminum officinale (summer jasmine) with variegated leaves, Trachelospermum jasminoïdes 'Variegatum', and Actinidia kolomikta with its handsome and unusual, tri-coloured leaves. Slow-growing Hedera helix varieties with coloured or variegated foliage are ideal for sun or shade.

Plant directory

Climbers

Climbing plants offer a wealth of ornamental attributes, not just from their flowers but also from attractively shaped or coloured foliage and decorative fruit. From the huge range of climbing plants available to the gardener today I have concentrated on selecting those which are of good ornamental value rather than making a complete list of every possible plant obtainable.

These plants climb in three different ways, and for the purposes of choosing the best type of support, or even whether one is needed at all, it's useful to know the plant's habit. Self-clinging ones, as their name suggests, fix themselves to a wall or fence with adhesive pads or aerial roots and need no support beyond some initial guidance in the right direction.

Twining plants wind their stems up a support such as wires or trellis, while plants with tendrils or twisting leaf stems will scramble happily up a mesh support or trellis with small spaces. All the plants listed below are deciduous unless stated otherwise. Sizes given are approximately those reached after ten years.

Actinidia kolomikta is a real stunner for unusual foliage colour, with slender, twining stems covered in heart-shaped, green leaves tipped with cream and pink, rather like a painter's palette. Cats often nibble at the leaves of this plant as for some reason they find its faint smell irresistible, so if necessary protect a new plant with netting until it has become well established. It does best in a moist yet well-drained soil, and prefers a south- or west-facing site. Height 3–4 m (10–13 ft). See page 118 for *Actinidia chinensis* (kiwi fruit).

Akebia quinata is a pretty climber which does best in a sheltered spot, as the blooms of this spring-flowering plant can be damaged by frost. Both flowers and foliage are attractive. The rich, reddish-purple, scented flowers nestle among a mass of delicate, five-lobed, fresh green leaves borne on slender, twining stems. The foliage sometimes stays on the plant through the winter. Height up to 4.5 m (15 ft).

Ampelopsis glandulosa var. *brevipedunculata* 'Elegans' is a name long enough to put anyone off, but the plant itself is very handsome, with lobed leaves that are heavily mottled with white and tinged with pink. It climbs by means of tendrils and is a slow, compact grower, reaching around 1.5 m (5 ft).

Aristolochia durior (Dutchman's pipe) tends to be grown as a curiosity for its unusual flowers, though its vigorous growth of large, heart-shaped leaves borne on twining stems is useful for clothing an old tree, for example, or covering the beams of a larger pergola. The brownish flowers have a curved, tubular calyx, not unlike an old clay pipe, and they appear in early summer. Height 4.5 m (15 ft).

Campsis (trumpet vine) is a magnificent and vigorous, sun-loving climber that bears clusters of gorgeously exotic, trumpet-shaped flowers at the ends of its stems in late summer or early autumn. The large, fresh green, jagged-edged leaves make a lovely background to the brightly coloured blooms. Choose from *Campsis radicans flava* 'Yellow Trumpet' with rich yellow flowers or *C. x tagliabuana* 'Madame Galen' which bears glowing orange-red ones. *Campsis* climbs by means of aerial roots, though it does best given some support. In cooler areas this plant tends to flower well only after a long, hot summer, and it is advisable not to put smaller plants in front of this climber as the whole plant needs to receive maximum sunshine to ground level. Height 4.5 m (15 ft).

Celastrus orbiculatus is a rampant, twining climber that is ideal for training up into a large tree, where it can form a cascade of foliage. Autumn is its season of glory, when the rounded, green leaves turn bright yellow and the seed capsules split open to reveal glowing orange-red seeds. To show off these autumn colours to best effect, grow it over a dark-foliaged tree such as a large conifer. Pollination must take place in order for seeds to be produced, so either plant a male and a female plant together or buy a hermaphrodite form with male and female flowers on the same plant. Height 4.5–6 m (15–20 ft).

Eccremocarpus: see page 113.

Hedera (ivy) is a greatly under-rated plant for the garden as the name tends to call to mind the common ivy with plain green leaves, rather than the many superb varieties with glossy, handsomely variegated foliage. Ivies are evergreen and they'll grow almost anywhere, in conditions varying from full sun to total shade, as well as being tolerant of poor soil, so they really are invaluable for year-round interest. They are self-clinging by means of aerial roots, which is an advantage in most cases, though it's advisable to avoid old walls where the mortar may be starting to crumble because the ivy will root into it and speed up the process of deterioration. It's best to keep ivy trimmed away from window frames and any other painted wood as the aerial roots are liable to cling onto the paintwork and damage it.

The two main species to choose from are *Hedera colchica* (Persian ivy), a vigorous, large-leaved species that can easily reach 5.1 m (17 ft), and *H. helix* which has smaller leaves and

~

Virginia creeper looks superb in autumn when its green leaves turn fiery red and drape this house front in curtains of flame.

grows up to 3.6 m (12 ft). Of the larger-leaved varieties, the most attractive ones include *H. colchica* 'Dentata Variegata', with green leaves that are strikingly edged with creamy-white, and *H. c.* 'Sulphur Heart' (also known as 'Paddy's Pride') that has dark green leaves with a bold central splash of pale lime-green.

There are numerous cultivars of the small-leaved *H. helix* species. Those with leaves that are completely green are the fastest-growing: they include *H. h.* 'Parsley Crested' (also known as 'Cristata') with rounded leaves that are crinkled at the edges, and *H. h.* 'Green Ripple' with small, jagged-edged leaves. Many ivies have leaves which are attractively variegated: those of 'Goldheart' are splashed with yellow, 'Luzii' is yellow marbled with green, and 'Glacier' has greyish-green leaves marked with white. 'Buttercup' is a bright lime-yellow, though it is slow-growing.

Hydrangea anomala **subsp.** *petiolaris* (climbing hydrangea) is a useful climber for a shady wall, though it can take several years to become established and start growing strongly. It is self-clinging, though it may need to be trained on to the wall in the first year or two. In summer a mass of fresh green leaves provides an ideal background for the large heads of cool white flowers, and the leaves turn yellow in autumn. Height 3 m (10 ft).

Jasminum officinale (summer or poet's jasmine) is a deciduous climber with twining stems, and it is one of the best plants of all for fragrance. Against a background of small,

dark green leaves, clusters of white flowers are borne from early summer through until autumn, giving off a delicious scent that is often strongest in the evening. The flowers of *J. o.* 'Affine' are slightly larger and tinged with pink. This species is happy in sun or shade, though flowers tend to be more freely produced in a sunny site. Prune in late winter by thinning out entire branches; do not shorten branches as this encourages lots of thin, bushy growth to be produced. Height 4 m (13 ft). *J.* x *stephanense* is a vigorous species bearing clusters of pale pink flowers in early to mid-summer. They are scented, though not as strongly as the blooms of *J. officinale*. Height up to 6 m (20 ft).

Varieties with colourful foliage are *J. o.* 'Aureum' and *J. o.* 'Argenteovariegatum', with leaves that are respectively variegated with gold and white. 'Fiona Sunrise' is a stunning new variety with leaves completely suffused with gold. They all bear flowers as well, though less profusely than the green-leaved species described above, and they need a reasonable amount of sunshine in order to bring out the best colour of their leaves. Height 2.4 m (8 ft).

Lonicera (honeysuckle) is another of the best scented climbers, and its fragrant flower clusters are a familiar sight in our gardens. Ideal for most sites, it prefers a well-drained soil with plenty of organic matter, with roots in the shade and its head in the sun. There is a wide range of species and cultivars from which to choose. All are twiners and most are decidu-ous, though there are a couple of varieties listed here which are evergreen in all but the hardest winters. Height approximately 4 m (13 ft).

The following honeysuckles are all deciduous. *Lonicera* x *americana* bears large heads of flowers which are rich rose-pink outside and pale yellow inside, in late summer and into autumn. *L. periclymenum* 'Belgica' (early Dutch honeysuckle) flowers in late spring and on into early summer, bearing clusters of reddish-purple-and-white flowers which fade to yellow. *L. p.* 'Serotina' (late Dutch honeysuckle) bears similar blooms from midsummer to autumn. *L. p.* 'Graham Thomas' has white flowers that later change to yellow. All these varieties have plain green leaves, while those of *L. p.* 'Harlequin' are prettily variegated in cream, pink and green. *L.* x *heckrottii* 'Goldflame' is a showy variety with large clusters of rich yellow flowers, flushed with orange, produced from early summer through into autumn.

Two honeysuckles that prefer full shade are *L.* x *tellmanniana* which has exceptionally handsome rich yellow flowers, flushed red in bud, borne in a massive display in early to mid-summer. *L. tragophylla* is even more spectacular with its long trumpets of golden-yellow flowers, though it can be difficult to obtain. Although gorgeous to look at, these species are not scented. Preferring sun but still lacking scent is *L.* x *brownii* 'Dropmore Scarlet', another showy form with glowing orange-red flowers.

Least fussy about site and soil is *L. japonica* 'Halliana' (Japanese honeysuckle), a rampant plant with semi-evergreen leaves that is ideal for covering or screening ugly objects. Let it loose on a length of unsightly chain-link fencing, for example, and in a short while the fence will be completely hidden. Many small clusters of sweetly scented, white-and-yellow flowers are borne from early summer to autumn, and birds love it as a nesting site. *L. j.* 'Aureoreticulata' is more compact and is grown for its golden variegated leaves rather than its flowers, and it is best given a reasonably sheltered site on good soil.

Parthenocissus species, which include the popular Virginia creeper or *P. quinquefolia*, are outstanding plants for fiery autumn colour. These vigorous plants are self-clinging, though they may need some initial training on to supports before they become attached. *Parthenocissus henryana* is the most ornamental one for summer interest, with three- to five-lobed, dark green leaves on which the veins are traced in silver. It is the least vigorous of the *Parthenocissus* species. *P. tricuspidata* 'Veitchii' (Boston ivy) also looks good in spring and summer, with small, jagged-edged, fresh green leaves. If growing these plants on a house wall, cut the stems back to about a metre (3 ft) below the guttering in winter or early spring so that they don't become tangled up and block the drainage. Height 4.8–9 m (16–30 ft).

Passiflora caerulea (passion flower) bears large, unusual flowers which make a real talking point. The parts of the flower are said to symbolize the instruments of the Crucifixion, with the three stigmas representing the three nails, the five anthers the five wounds, and so on. This interest apart, the

A sunny, sheltered wall creates a warm microclimate which is ideal for slightly tender shrubs like this beautiful Abutilon x suntense.

~

passion flower is a lovely climber for a sunny spot, quickly scrambling up by means of tendrils and covering its support with attractive, lobed dark green leaves. The blue-and-white flowers are borne sporadically through summer, and if there have been long spells of hot weather, orange, egg-shaped fruits may be produced, the seeds and the pulp of which are edible. The variety 'Constance Elliott' has beautiful, pure ivory-white flowers.

Passion flowers prefer a well-drained soil, and though they are hardy in all but the most severe winters, sometimes the foliage can be cut to ground level by hard frosts. However, they usually regrow swiftly in spring. Mulching the base of the plant with straw will help protect the roots from the worst frosts. Height 4.8 m (16 ft). There are also a number of other passion flowers which are generally suitable only for conservatory use or for a sheltered spot in the mildest areas. See page 116.

Pileostegia viburnoïdes is a useful, self-clinging, evergreen climber that does well in sun or shade, in any good garden soil. The pointed, bright green leaves have a leathery texture and make a good background to the creamy-white, fluffy heads of flowers that are borne in late summer and into autumn. Height 3-4 m (10-13 ft).

Polygonum baldschuanicum (now renamed *Fallopia baldschuanica*), the Russian vine, is one species that I feel should be planted only after severe consideration because its speed of growth is legendary. The plant is definitely not called mile-a-minute for nothing! Its vigour wouldn't be so bad if the plant were attractive, but its small, plain green leaves have nothing really to commend them, and the panicles of white flowers in early summer aren't particularly beautiful. This is not a plant for the average garden, unless you want to cover up an old building. Height and spread 7 m (23 ft).

Solanum has a less-than-appealing common name of potato flower, though its two main species are handsome and excellent garden plants that do best in full sun. *Solanum crispum* 'Glasnevin' is half-way between a shrub and a climber, with long, arching branches that are covered with blue-mauve, orange-centred flowers from early to late summer, and often through into autumn. *S. jasminoides* 'Album' is a delightful plant with twining stems, bearing clusters of elegant, pure white flowers that have a central sheaf of golden stamens. These are displayed against a background of glossy, dark green leaves from early summer until autumn. Height 4.8 m (16 ft).

Trachelospermum is a choice and lovely plant with jasmine-like flowers that have a delicious scent. It is neat and well-behaved, with self-clinging stems clothed with small, glossy, dark green leaves and flowers that are borne from mid- to late summer. However, it does need the protection of a sunny, sheltered wall in order to come through the winter unscathed in all but mild areas. Of the two species which are generally available, *Trachelospermum asiaticum* is the hardiest, with creamy-white, yellow-centred flowers that age completely to yellow. The flowers of *T. jasminoïdes* are white, turning to cream. There is a handsome variegated form *T. j.* 'Variegatum', with leaves edged and splashed with creamy-white, sometimes also flushed with pink in winter.

Prune in spring if it is necessary to contain any vigorous growth. Height 2.4–3 m (8–10 ft).

Vitis (ornamental vines) are vigorous tendril climbers with large, handsome leaves. One of the best species is *Vitis coignetiae*, an exceptionally large-leaved plant with leaves up to 30 cm (12 in) long, which develop superb, long-lasting autumn tints of crimson and scarlet. Most ornamental of the grapevines is *V. vinifera* 'Purpurea' (claret vine) with lobed leaves that are faintly tinted with purple earlier in the season, the colour gradually deepening towards the autumn until the whole plant becomes a blaze of colour. Small bunches of black-purple grapes contrast well with the leaves. There are several other less common vines which are grown principally for their attractive foliage. *V. davidii* has large, heart-shaped, toothed leaves which are a handsome dark green on top and glaucous underneath and in autumn they turn a beautiful shade of rich crimson.

Any necessary pruning is best done in winter. Height 4.5–7 m (15–23 ft). For fruiting vines see page 117.

Wisteria is a superb and aristocratic plant for a sunny spot, though it does take a few years to become sufficiently well established to produce a good show of its long, dangling racemes of flowers. These magnificent blooms, borne in late spring to early summer, have a delectable coconut-like scent, and the large, pinnate leaves bring an oriental air to the garden.

Blue-flowered varieties are by far the most popular, though there are white- and pink-flowered types too. Most vigorous is *Wisteria sinensis* (Chinese wisteria), which can grow up to 7 m (23 ft) and considerably more in time, while *W. floribunda* and *W. formosa* are more compact, growing to around 4–5 m (13–17 ft). Good varieties include *W. fo.* 'Domino' with dark blue flowers and *W. fl.* 'Multijuga' that has larger-than-average racemes of pale blue flowers. In colder areas plant wisteria against a sheltered, south-facing wall, as the buds can be damaged by late spring frosts.

To encourage flower production, prune wisteria twice a year. In summer thin out overcrowded side shoots and cut the remaining ones back to about 15 cm (6 in). The following winter cut these same shoots again back to two or three buds. Feeding with sulphate of potash in late winter also helps boost flowering. Avoid feeding wisteria with high-nitrogen fertilizer which will encourage leafy growth at the expense of flowers.

Wall shrubs

The range of plants for walls and fences can be broadened even further with the addition of wall shrubs. This is a group of plants that can be trained on to walls, fences or frameworks by tying their stems to horizontal wires or trellis. In many cases the plant can be kept almost flat against its support if all outward-facing shoots are pruned out and new ones regularly tied in. Some plants are susceptible to frost damage in colder areas and they really benefit from the storage-heater effect of a sheltered, south-facing wall which will usually protect them from harm in all but the most severe of winters.

If you live in a very cold area and want to grow some of these potentially tender wall plants, a little extra protection can make all the difference to their survival. It's useful to prepare the material in advance. Cut a piece of polythene or sacking that is sufficiently large to cover your plant and fix a long piece of wood to each end. This enables the material to be easily rolled up and stored when not required, yet it can be unrolled and put over the plant within minutes when necessary.

All sizes of plants given are approximately those reached after ten years. However, size can vary according to the type and fertility of the soil and the warmth or otherwise of the climate.

Abutilon brings a distinctly exotic flavour to the garden with its stunning, brightly coloured flowers. *A. megapotamicum* and hybrids such as 'Kentish Belle' both bear dangling, bell-shaped flowers that have a rich, deep red base and yellow or apricot petals. The blooms of *A.* x *suntense* are saucer-shaped and a lovely shade of lavender-blue. Height 1.8–2.4 m (6–8 ft).

Aloysia triphylla syn. *Lippia citriodora* (lemon verbena) is a must for lovers of fragrant foliage. Its slender, fresh green leaves give off a sharp and delicious lemon scent when crushed. They are excellent for drying and using in pot-pourri, and for making herbal tea. Small and rather insignificant panicles of mauve flowers are borne in summer. It is susceptible to frost damage, so it needs a sunny, very sheltered spot. Alternatively you can grow this plant in a large pot and over-winter it in an unheated greenhouse. Height 1.5 m (5 ft).

Berberidopsis corallina (coral plant) is an unusual shrub that is beautiful in flower, bearing drooping clusters of shiny, globe-shaped, crimson blooms in late summer or early autumn. The evergreen leaves are toothed at the edges and dark green. However, this plant is choosy about its growing conditions and is best grown only in milder areas. It needs a cool, shady, yet sheltered site and a deep acid soil that is rich in organic matter. Height 1.8 m (6 ft).

Ceanothus (Californian lilac) includes many magnificent species and hybrids that mostly bear flowers which are an exquisite, almost unreal shade of blue. Susceptible to winter frost damage in colder areas, they thrive

The Californian lilac or Ceanothus *have flowers that are a beautiful and almost unreal shade of blue. This one is* C. impressus.

~

against a sunny, sheltered wall where their growth tends to bush outwards for a metre (3 ft) or more. *Ceanothus* need a well-drained soil, though they dislike chalky ground. Height and spread 1.8–3 m (6–10 ft).

Some of the best and hardiest of the hybrids and species are 'Delight', 'Edinburgh', 'Puget Blue' and *C. thyrsiflorus*, which flower in spring or early summer, and 'Autumnal Blue' that blooms in late summer. They are all evergreen. Less hardy hybrids include 'A.T. Johnson', which flowers in spring and autumn, while 'Cascade' and 'Italian Skies' bloom in spring. There are also several pink, summer-flowering *Ceanothus*, such as *C.* x *pallidus* 'Marie Simon' with pale pink flowers and *C. p.* 'Perle Rose' that is deep pink. Both of these hybrids are deciduous.

Chaenomeles (flowering quince or japonica) is an easily grown shrub that thrives in either sun or shade, on all except chalky soils. It bears many blooms all along its naked branches in early spring, followed in autumn by edible fruits that can be used in preserves.

There are many named varieties producing flowers in a wide range of colours, such as *C. speciosa* 'Apple Blossom' (also known as 'Moerloosei') which is blush pink, the pure white *C. s.* 'Nivalis', *C. s.* 'Umbilicata' which is coral-pink and *C. x superba* 'Knap Hill Scarlet' which bears brilliant orange-red flowers. Height 1.8 m (6 ft).

Cotoneaster horizontalis (herring-bone cotoneaster) is a go-anywhere, do-anything plant that flourishes in all but the poorest of soils, in sun or shade. Though it is more commonly used as a ground-cover plant, it will happily ramble up a wall if it is pointed in the right direction to begin with. In fact I prefer this plant when it grows upwards, as the handsome fish-bone shape of its branches is much more apparent against the background of a wall or fence. Many clusters of small, white flowers are borne in spring, followed by bright red berries strung all along its branches. The small, oval leaves also turn glowing red before falling. Height 1.8 m (6 ft).

Cytisus battandieri (pineapple or Moroccan broom) needs plenty of room, both in front and to the sides, to throw out its long stems. Cone-shaped clusters of yellow flowers, which have a delicious pineapple scent, are borne in early summer. The foliage is particularly handsome, being rather like that of a laburnum but silvery-grey in colour. Height and spread 2.4–3 m (8–10 ft).

Eriobotrya japonica (loquat) is one of the best evergreens for bold, architectural foliage effect against a sunny wall, with its leathery, corrugated leaves that can each be up to 30 cm (12 in) long. Clusters of white, strongly scented flowers may be borne in mild areas or after a hot summer, opening from late winter through to spring. In very favourable sites, edible yellow fruits may also be produced. Height and spread 3–4.5 m (10–15 ft).

Escallonia is an attractive flowering evergreen that bears masses of small, tubular flowers in summer. Of the many good hybrids, some of the best include 'Apple Blossom' with pink and white flowers, 'C.F. Ball' which is crimson, the rose-red 'Donard Radiance' and 'Iveyi' which has pure white

~

Cape figwort or Phygelius *has exotic-looking tubular flowers which are borne on tall stems over a long period from mid to late summer.*

flowers. Two newer varieties, 'Gold Brian' and 'Gold Ellen', have large, deep gold leaves and a compact habit. Although escallonias tend to become very bushy if left unpruned, they can easily be kept in shape by pruning as necessary after flowering. They thrive in any well-drained soil in a sunny position and do particularly well near the sea. Height and spread up to 2.4 m (8 ft).

Euonymus fortunei cultivars are commonly used for ground cover, but these trailing evergreens will happily, if slowly, ramble upwards, gradually forming a self-clinging curtain of bright foliage that is particularly appreciated in winter. Good cultivars include 'Silver Queen' whose leaves are boldly variegated with green and white, 'Variegatus' with green, white-edged leaves sometimes tinged with pink, and 'Coloratus' whose green leaves are handsomely coloured with reddish-purple in the winter. They grow well in sun or shade. Height 1.5 m (5 ft).

Fremontodendron 'California Glory' is a magnificent sight in summer covered with waxy-petalled, golden, saucer-shaped flowers that can be up to 7 cm (3 in) across. The large, lobed, grey-green leaves are evergreen and covered with tiny hairs; beware these and the brown seed capsules, which can irritate the skin and eyes if handled. It needs a sunny, sheltered site and well-drained soil. Height and spread 3.6 m (12 ft).

Garrya is a useful evergreen shrub that, although unremarkable in its foliage, looks superb in winter when it bears long tassels of grey-green catkins. *G. elliptica* is the most widely available species, and it is worth seeking out the cultivar 'James Roof' that bears extra-large catkins up to 20 cm (8 in) long. This plant is particularly useful for a shady as well as a sunny site, so long as it isn't too exposed to cold winter winds. Height and spread up to 3 m (10 ft).

Jasminum nudiflorum (winter jasmine) is wonderfully cheering in the depths of winter, covered with masses of starry, bright yellow flowers. Even better, this plant is tough and easily pleased, so it can be grown in shade or sun, against a wall or up a post or pergola. Prune immediately after flowering by cutting all the flowered shoots back to two or three buds from the main stem. Height 1.8 m (6 ft).

Magnolia grandiflora is a stately, elegant shrub that needs both space and patience. In time it will cover a large expanse of wall with its massive, glossy, evergreen leaves, though to begin with it will usually take a few years before it produces the first of its huge, waxy petalled, pure white blooms. Avoid plants that have been raised from seed, because they can take many years to flower. Choose named varieties such as the excellent 'Goliath', or one of the newer varieties that have been selected for their tendency to flower early in their life, such as 'Saint Mary', 'Russet' and 'Samuel Sommer'. These magnolias need a sunny wall in order to give of their best. Height and spread 3.6 m (12 ft).

Phygelius (Cape figwort) can be treated as a herbaceous plant and grown in the border, but it gains enormously in height and quality when grown against a wall. Tall stems are clothed with exotic, tubular, brightly coloured flowers from mid-summer until the first frosts. Good varieties include *P. aequalis* 'Yellow Trumpet' that is deep butter-yellow, *P. capensis coccineus* which has red flowers, and 'Salmon Leap' whose blooms are bright orange. They do best in sun but tolerate a fair amount of shade, on any reasonable soil. In spring prune the whole plant to 30 cm (12 in). Height 1.8 m (6 ft), spread 60 cm (24 in).

Piptanthus nepalensis (evergreen laburnum) is handsome in both flower and foliage, and this shrub deserves to be grown more widely. The glossy, three-lobed, dark green leaves are evergreen in all but the hardest winters, and they make a good background for the spikes of bright yellow flowers that are borne in early summer. If any pruning is necessary, do it immediately after flowering. In colder areas give this shrub the protection of a sunny, sheltered wall. Height 1.8–2.4 m (6–8 ft).

Pyracantha (firethorn) is a vigorous, easily grown shrub that gives interest in both spring and autumn. First it bears clusters of white, hawthorn-like flowers in late spring, followed in autumn by bunches of colourful berries. There is a number of varieties with different berry colours. Yellow-fruiting ones include 'Golden Charmer' and 'Soleil d'Or' (also known as 'Golden Sun'), those with orange berries include 'Orange Glow' and 'Orange Charmer', while *P. coccinea* 'Red Column' and *P. atalantioides* bear red berries. Scab disease, which disfigures the leaves and berries, can be a problem with pyracanthas. Some varieites are resistant to scab, and these ones should be planted if the disease has been a nuisance in the past. Two new, disease-resistant varieties are 'Saphyr Red' and 'Saphyr Orange', with names that refer to the colour of their berries. This shrub is immensely popular with birds, not just for a feast of autumn berries – they prefer red and orange ones – but also because the dense growth and prickly stems make ideal nesting sites. Height 3.6 m (12 ft).

Teucrium fruticans (shrubby germander) has small, handsome, grey-green leaves that make a lovely background for its clusters of pale blue flowers. They are borne through summer and are very popular with bees. This is a slightly tender plant which benefits from a sunny, sheltered wall and a free-draining soil. Height 1.5 m (5 ft).

Viburnum x *burkwoodii* is a handsome shrub with semi-evergreen leaves which are glossy green on top and felted underneath. Heads of sweetly scented white flowers, tinged with green or pink, are borne for several weeks in spring. *V.* x *b.* 'Park Farm Hybrid' is a selected form with larger flowers and with a slightly more spreading habit than the species. This plant forms a large, rather open bush and it can be trained against its support by pruning outward facing buds. Height 2.4 m (8 ft).

Clematis

Whatever the place in the garden, there is bound to be a clematis that is suitable to fill it. This immensely versatile group of plants comprises an enormous range of species and hybrids in a wealth of colours, so there really is something for everyone. Indeed, by selecting a range of different varieties, it's possible to have clematis in flower almost every month of the year, though the best time for a real bonanza of blooms is through late spring to the middle of summer.

With so many superb varieties from which to choose, the difficulty is deciding just which ones to grow. Clematis broadly divide into two main groups: the large-flowered hybrids with blooms up to 20 cm (8 in) across, and a number of different species and their hybrids which, although their flowers are smaller, more than make up for it by producing them in larger numbers and often over a longer period.

Of these two groups the large-flowered hybrids need the better growing conditions in order to give of their best, while the majority of the species are a lot tougher and much more tolerant of adverse conditions. The hybrids are generally the least vigorous of the two groups, which makes them ideal for all sorts of places – in containers and up free-standing supports, as well as on walls and fences, either on their own or mixed in with other plants. Indeed it is their suitability for doubling up with other plants that makes them one of the most useful of all climbing plants. These clematis can be grown through established plants such as shrubs, conifers or trees, to give an extra burst of contrasting summer colour. Choose the flower colour that looks best against the chosen background – deep blue flowers against silver foliage, for example, or pure white against a dark green conifer. Double-flowered varieties benefit greatly from being grown through another plant, as the weight of their blooms can cause the stems to bend down or even break.

~

Many clematis make ideal partners for other plants, because they are not over-vigorous. Here the deep blue flowers of Clematis *'Royalty' contrast well with the golden leaflets of* Robinia *'Frisia'.*

There are now so many different clematis available that I have dealt only with those varieties that are, in the main, fairly easy to obtain. However, if you become smitten by these beautiful plants – which can happen very easily – there is a number of excellent specialist nurseries that grow an enormous range of less usual varieties along with all the better-known ones.

Large-flowered hybrids

Site and soil

The large-flowered hybrids prefer a site sheltered from strong winds. They do best when given a deep, moisture-retentive soil rich in organic matter, and ideally one that is neutral or alkaline (limy) rather than acid. They also like to have their roots in the shade and their 'heads' in the sun, and often the easiest way

A few clematis need the protection of a sunny wall, such as C. armandii, *a handsome evergreen which is smothered in scented white flowers in spring.*

~

to provide such conditions is to put them in a sunny spot and to shade the roots with large stones or ground-cover plants. However, with a few exceptions, both species and hybrid clematis thrive in sun or shade. Indeed some large-flowered hybrids actually do better in a shady spot, notably those with pale, bi-coloured flowers like 'Nelly Moser' and 'Bee's Jubilee' which bear pink-and-white blooms, because more than a little sunlight will cause their delicate colouring to fade. If conditions are less than ideal, it is generally better to opt for species clematis instead of the large-flowered hybrids.

The following varieties are a selection of the most popular ones from the considerable range available. They range in height from 2.4–3.6 m (8–12 ft).

Whites and creams

These pale shades look good almost anywhere in the garden. Grow them through evergreen shrubs with dark, glossy foliage, or in a shady corner where the flowers will lighten the gloom. 'Marie Boisselot' (also known as 'Madame le Coultre') is one of the best and most reliable varieties, with pure white flowers. 'John Huxtable' is white with cream stamens. Some varieties such as 'Edith', 'Henryi' and 'Miss Bateman' have dark stamens that contrast beautifully with their pale blooms. 'Silver Moon' is an unusual shade of pearly-grey, while 'Guernsey Cream' is creamy-yellow.

Double-flowered varieties include 'Arctic Queen' (pure white), 'Duchess of Edinburgh' (white with yellow stamens) and 'Mrs George Jackman' (creamy-white with dark stamens).

Blues and purples

Blues and purples are the most popular clematis flower colours. There are many stunning shades that range from lavender-blue to rich, vibrant purple. Blue flowers look good with yellow and pink blooms and contrast well with silver and variegated foliage. Violet and purple clematis are superbly set off against a background of pale leaves, as well as looking equally good with purple or coppery foliage.

Good varieties include 'William Kennett' (lavender-blue), 'Lasurstern' which is a richer shade of the same colour, the beautiful sky-blue 'Perle d'Azur', and 'The President' which is purple-blue. Darkest of all are the rich purple tones of 'Jackmanii Superba'.

Varieties with contrasting stamens look particularly handsome: they include 'Haku-ôkan' (violet-blue with white stamens), 'H.F. Young' (Wedgwood blue with cream stamens) and 'Mrs P.B. Truax' (clear blue with cream stamens).

Double-flowered varieties include 'Beauty of Worcester' with deep blue flowers, 'Countess of Lovelace' which is lavender-blue, the purple-blue 'Multi Blue', 'Royalty' which is purple-mauve and 'Vyvyan Pennell' which has violet-blue blooms.

Pinks and reds

Darker shades make a startling contrast to gold and silver foliage and they look good in 'hot' colour schemes of red and purple flowers. The pinks are altogether softer and harmonize well with pink and mauve flowers, as well as with purple foliage.

Good pinks include 'Comtesse de Bouchaud' (pinky-mauve), 'Hagley Hybrid' (pale pink), 'Peveril Pearl' (pale lilac-pink) and 'Pink Fantasy' (deep pink with a slightly deeper bar). 'Mrs Spencer Castle' bears pale pink-mauve, double flowers. Darker pinks and reds include 'Ernest Markham' (petunia-red), 'Niobe' (rich ruby-red), 'Rouge Cardinal' (crimson) and 'Ville de Lyon' (carmine-red).

Note. If you are growing any of the double-flowered clematis, bear in mind that it is not unusual for single blooms to be produced, particularly during the latter part of the season or when the plant is young.

Striped flowers

In addition to the many single-coloured clematis varieties, there are a number that have a central stripe of a different colour down the centre of each sepal. They include 'Nelly Moser' and 'Bees' Jubilee' (pale mauve-pink with a deep pink bar), 'Barbara Jackman' (blue-purple with a carmine bar), 'Pink Champagne' (pink with a pale bar), 'Scartho Gem' (bright pink with a deeper stripe), and 'Mrs N. Thompson' (deep violet with a bright pink bar).

Clematis wilt

Clematis wilt is the main disease to which clematis are prone, and generally it is only the large-flowered hybrids that tend to be susceptible. The symptoms are immediately apparent when all or part of a plant suddenly wilts and collapses. At first glance the plant appears to be suffering from lack of water, but the affected parts will not recover and they will eventually die.

Although there is no cure, several measures can be taken to give the plant a good chance of recovery. When planting, put the top of the rootball several centimetres lower than the level at which it was growing previously, as this enables the plant to produce stems from below ground level. Should it then suffer from clematis wilt, the affected parts can be cut back to ground level and there is a good chance that fresh stems will eventually be produced. However, as is the case with many diseases, healthy plants are much more resistant to attack. So good ground preparation, coupled with regular feeding and watering plus an annual mulch of organic matter, will keep the plant growing strongly.

Lastly, don't be too hasty to dig out an apparently dead clematis. They can be slow to recover, and the plant may not produce new shoots for six months or even longer.

Clematis species

C. alpina and *C. macropetala* are two charming and beautiful species which will cheer up the garden in early spring. The fresh young foliage appears early in the season, soon to be followed by many nodding heads of flowers. Blue-flowered forms such as *C. alpina* 'Pamela Jackman' and 'Frances Rivis' and *C. macropetala* 'Blue Bird' are most popular, though there are pink and white forms too. As these species are not over-vigorous, with slender stems that grow to around 2.4 m (8 ft) high, they are ideal for small gardens and for partnering with other plants. My favourite combination is a blue variety with a variegated evergreen such as the large-leaved ivy *Hedera colchica* 'Dentata Variegata'.

C. armandii is one of the few evergreen clematis, and its large, leathery, dark green leaves make a perfect foil for the large clusters of pale, fragrant flowers that are borne in spring. Two excellent varieties are 'Snowdrift' which is a pure, brilliant white, while the flowers of 'Apple Blossom' are flushed with pink. In colder areas this plant really needs the protection of a sunny wall in order to avoid becoming disfigured or even killed by severe frosts. Height 3.6–4.5 m (12–15 ft).

C. cirrhosa is also evergreen, though this is definitely a plant for a sheltered wall in all but the mildest areas. It also prefers a well-drained soil. As well as its small, attractive leaves that become tinged with bronze in winter, its real charm is in the bell-shaped blooms borne in winter and early spring when few other climbers are in flower. The ivory-white flowers are plain in the case of 'Wisley Cream', otherwise they are splashed and spotted with red inside, this colouring being more pronounced in the case of the variety 'Freckles'. The most attractive foliage belongs to *C. c. balearica* (fern-leaved clematis), so called because its leaves are more divided than those of the species. Height 3.6–4.5 m (12–15 ft).

C. x durandii is semi-herbaceous in habit, which means that although its slender, sprawling stems cannot be left to climb unsupported, it is perfect to grow through a small shrub or to sprawl over a low, ground-covering plant. The deep Wedgwood-blue flowers look superb against the golden foliage of the shrub *Elaeagnus pungens* 'Maculata', for example, or a yellow-leaved juniper. Height 1.2–1.8 m (4–6 ft).

Clematis montana is just about the most rampant of all the species, though any over-enthusiastic tendencies can be forgiven in late spring when the whole plant is dripping with beautiful, pure white, four petalled blooms. It

is extremely vigorous, easily reaching 6–9 m (20–30 ft), which makes it ideal for growing over an old building. A large, established tree also makes an ideal host and it's a good idea to choose an evergreen such as holly or a large green conifer, because the pale blooms show up so well against a dark background

Clematis *'Jackmanii Alba' is a vigorous hybrid bearing masses of beautiful white blooms.*

and the year-round foliage of the host plant mostly hides the ropes of bare clematis stems in winter.

As well as the species, another white form is *C. m.* 'Alexander' that has slightly larger and fragrant flowers. The pink-flowered varieties are exceptionally lovely too, such as

C. m. 'Elizabeth' with pale pink blooms, and *C. m.* 'Rubens' which is a slightly deeper shade. The flowers of *C. m.* 'Tetrarose' are a pretty shade of lilac-pink.

Although no regular pruning is required, this plant is often placed in a site where there isn't enough room to grow and so a severe 'haircut' is needed every couple of years. In such a case prune immediately after flowering, because the next spring's flowers will be borne on the growth that will be made during the coming summer.

C. orientalis and **C. tangutica** are yellow, a rare colour among clematis. They have the additional bonus of flowering late in the summer too, filling that awkward gap that can occur in the garden at this time. Yellow, lantern-shaped flowers are borne among divided, sea-green leaves, followed by attractive, fluffy seed heads that, as the flowers are produced over a number of weeks, are joined by the blooms that appear towards the end of the season. I like to grow these clematis over an archway or pergola, where the harvest-gold flowers can be seen against the clear blue of an autumn sky. Height 2.4–3 m (8–10 ft). No regular pruning is required, but if the plant has got out of hand and has developed into a tangled mass of shoots, it can be hard pruned to within 60 cm (24 in) of the ground in late winter or early spring.

C. texensis is a charming species that benefits from the protection of a sunny wall in colder areas. Its lovely, bell-shaped flowers appear in late summer, in a variety of richly

Clematis viticella *hybrids are immensely useful as they can be cut almost to the ground in spring, so they are perfect with other plants. This one is* C.v. *'Purpurea Plena Elegans'.*

coloured shades. Those of 'Duchess of Albany' are deep pink with a red band, the blooms of 'Etoile Rose' are edged with silvery-pink, while those of 'Gravetye Beauty' are ruby-red and expand outwards to form a star shape. Height 1.8–3 m (6–10 ft).

C. viticella is perhaps the most versatile of all the species clematis. This is due not only to its speedy production of slender stems, which enable it to be grown through and over lots of different plants, but also because it benefits from being treated almost like a herbaceous plant. Every year in late winter or early spring the whole plant is best cut back to within 45 cm (18 in) of the ground, from where it will quickly produce stems up to 3 m (10 ft) long. Masses of flowers are borne over a long period from mid- to late summer and into autumn.

The many excellent hybrids come in a wide range of flower colours. They include 'Abundance' (rose-pink), 'Alba Luxurians' (white), 'Etiole Violette' (violet), 'Minuet' (white veined with mauve) and 'Polish Spirit' (bright red). Flower shapes vary from an open flower of four petals to a nodding bell-shape with the petals curving back at the tips. In addition there is a double form, 'Purpurea Plena Elegans' with little violet-purple rosettes of flowers.

How to prune clematis

Because clematis fall into three different groups for pruning purposes, there can be confusion over how to treat a particular plant. However, it is quite straightforward so long as you check when your plant flowers. If you know the name of your clematis, simply look up its pruning group in a specialist book on clematis, or obtain a catalogue from a specialist nursery. When in doubt, leave your plant unpruned until it flowers and you can identify the variety or species.

Group 1 clematis flower in spring and early summer, so the flowers are borne on growth that was made the previous summer. This group includes *C. alpina*, *C. macropetala* and *C. montana*, as well as a number of early-bloom-ing, large-flowered hybrids. Little pruning is needed apart from removing dead and weak stems after flowering. Overgrown plants can be pruned hard at the same time if necessary.

Group 2 clematis flower from early to mid-summer, and they also flower on last year's growth. This group includes many of the large-flowered hybrids. Cut out dead and weak stems after flowering, and prune the remaining ones back to a strong pair of buds.

Group 3 clematis flower late in the season on growth produced in spring and summer. This group includes clematis species such as *C. orientalis* and *C. viticella,* and vigorous, large-flowered hybrids such as 'Gipsy Queen' and 'Jackmanii Superba'. In early spring cut all growth back to about 30–45 cm (12–18 in) from ground level.

Roses

Roses are invaluable for providing a wealth of luxuriant colour in the summer garden, and their beautiful blooms often have a rich perfume too. There is a vast range of varieties from which to choose and the sheer number of these can easily fill an entire book. For this reason I have concentrated on providing some general advice on rose-growing along with details on the main plant groups and a limited selection of varieties.

Roses do best in full sun on a fertile, well-drained soil, so it's best to avoid ground that can become waterlogged, soil that is exceptionally chalky, or damp, acid peat. A few climbers will tolerate shade (see page 108).

Roses are hungry plants and they really benefit from an annual spring mulch of well-rotted compost or manure, as well as repeated dressings of fertilizer. Keeping roses in good condition with regular feeding, mulching, and watering during dry spells, makes them less susceptible to attacks of pests and diseases. Prevention, as opposed to the use of harmful chemicals, is far better for the overall health of your garden and its natural inhabitants, particularly as many insects and creatures will combat pests for you.

In order to be sure of having the right rose for a particular site, it's useful to outline the main differences between climbing and rambler roses. Climbers form a main framework of rigid branches from which come the smaller side shoots that produce flowers. The main branches are best trained fan-wise or horizontally to restrict the flow of sap slightly, which therefore boosts the number of flowers produced. Hence climbing roses are best suited to walls, fences and frameworks, though compact, modern varieties of climbing rose are suitable for training up pillars and posts. Rambler roses, on the other hand, produce long, flexible shoots, mostly from the base of the plant, and so they are more suited to arbours, arches and pergolas than climbing roses. They also look very good when grown informally: through an established tree or over a shed, for example, where the long stems provide a cascade of blooms.

For the purpose of individual tastes, it's useful to distinguish between the flower types and flowering times of these two groups. Climbing roses have comparatively large flowers, often borne in repeated flushes through the summer, while ramblers produce clusters of small, sometimes tiny blooms in great profusion for a period of several weeks.

When you come to buy your plants, bear in mind that most garden centres have space for only a limited range of varieties, but there is a number of specialist nurseries that supply an exceptionally good range of roses by mail order. Plants are despatched during the winter while they are dormant, and it's a good idea to place your order earlier in the year to be sure of securing your first choices. Choosing a few roses from all the varieties available can be extremely difficult, but one good way to pick out your favourites is to visit a specialist rose garden or nursery in the summer. Here it's usually possible to see mature plants, often growing in a garden situation, so assessing a variety for eventual size and flower colour becomes much easier. If scent is high on your list of priorities, there is really no substitute for first-hand inspection, particularly as the fragrance of a rose can vary from a fresh apple scent to a rich, heady perfume. Of course, there are also many roses that have no scent at all. In any case there are few more pleasant ways to pass a couple of hours on a sunny summer's afternoon.

Pruning

Climbers and ramblers are pruned in totally different ways, and this also influences their suitability for a certain site.

Prune climbing roses in early spring by shortening the side shoots to about 15 cm (6 in). Leave the main framework untouched unless the plant is outgrowing its site, in

Rosa 'Zéphirine Drouhin' is a lovely old-fashioned variety with fragrant flowers. It is susceptible to mildew, but its near-thornless stems ensure this rose remains a firm favourite with gardeners.

which case shorten the shoots as required. If the base of an old rose has become very bare, one or two main stems can be cut back almost to the ground to encourage new growth.

Prune rambler roses in late summer immedi-ately after flowering. The easiest method is to untie the shoots and lay them on the ground. Prune out about a third to a half of the old, flowered stems at ground level, then tie the remaining growths back on their support.

For both climbers and ramblers cut out all weak, dead, diseased and damaged shoots first. If in doubt as to the identity of your rose, just restrict your pruning to this, rather than risk cutting off a season's flowers by mistake.

Climbing roses

Old-fashioned climbers

Many of the old-fashioned climbing roses bear reasonably large, rosette-type flowers that often have a delicious fragrance. They include climbing forms of Bourbon roses, which often repeat flower well, and Noisette roses, which are free-flowering though they generally benefit from the pro-tection of a sheltered wall, as do climbing Tea roses. Popular varieties include 'Gloire de Dijon' (buff-yellow flushed with pink),

'Lady Hillingdon' (apricot-yellow), 'Madame Alfred Carrière' (white flushed pink) and 'Zéphirine Drouhin' (deep rose-pink). However, some old varieties can be susceptible to disease, so it's worth checking this out in advance.

Modern climbers

Modern climbing roses mostly have a compact habit, growing to around 2.4–3 m (8–10 ft) high, and they do well on pillars, walls and trellis. Their flowers are similar to those of a Hybrid Tea rose in character, being reasonably large and also flowering in repeat flushes through summer. Many modern roses also have good disease resistance. Good varieties include 'Aloha' (rose-pink), 'Breath of Life' (apricot-pink), 'Casino' (yellow), 'Compassion' (salmon-pink tinged with apricot), 'Danse de Feu' (bright red), 'Dreamgirl' (coral-pink), 'Golden Showers' (yellow), 'Handel' (white with pink and red markings), 'Maigold' (bronze-yellow), 'Pink Perpétué' (bright rose-pink), 'Parkdirektor Riggers' (single, deep red), 'Schoolgirl' (apricot), 'Swan Lake' (white flushed with pale pink) and 'White Cockade' (pure white).

Climbing Floribunda and Hybrid Tea roses are sports of well-known bush roses such as 'Ena Harkness' (red), 'Iceberg' (white) and 'Masquerade' (yellow-red). They range in size from about 3 to 6 m (10 to 20 ft).

Of recent introduction are several miniature

The blooms of Rosa *'New Dawn' have a faint but delicious apple scent.*

climbers that grow only to around 1.8 m (6 ft) high, which makes them ideal for small gardens and large containers. They are 'Laura Ford' (amber yellow), 'Little Rambler', (blush pink), 'Nice Day' (pale salmon-pink), 'Rosalie Coral' (orange-yellow) and 'Warm Welcome' (bright orange).

Although climbing roses are most successful in a sunny site, a few varieties will do reasonably well in a shady site such as a north wall. They include 'Danse de Feu', 'Gloire de Dijon', 'Golden Showers', 'Madame Alfred Carrière', 'New Dawn' and 'Zéphirine Drouhin'.

Rambler roses

The blooms of rambler roses range from almost thimble-size to about 10 cm (4 in) across. They are borne in large clusters in one magnificent flush lasting for several weeks. Heights range from approximately 4 to 6 m (13 to 20 ft) with the exception of a few very vigorous varieties that are covered separately (see below).

Good varieties include 'Albéric Barbier' (creamy white), 'Albertine' (pink flushed yellow), 'Crimson Shower' (bright crimson), 'Debutante' (rose-pink), 'Emily Gray' (gold-yellow), 'Félicité et Perpétue' (creamy-white flushed pink), 'Madame de Sancy de Parabère' (soft pink), 'Mountain Snow' (white semi-double flowers with golden anthers) and 'Sander's White' (pure white).Several varieties (eg, 'Frances E. Lester' and 'Rambling Rector') have a tendency to form a bushy mass of growth and may also be grown as large shrubs.

Vigorous ramblers and climbing rose species

It is worth making the distinction between these ultra-vigorous varieties and those previously mentioned because of their eventual and considerable size of 7.3–15.2 m (25–50 ft). This makes them suitable for only a few locations in the garden, such as a large, established tree, a good-size outbuilding, the entire front of an average house or a substantial wooden framework. However, where such roses can be given free rein, they do make a superb and breathtaking display of flowers. The following species and varieties are most generally available.

Rosa brunonii bears large clusters of fragrant, white flowers among handsome grey-green foliage. *R. b.* 'La Mortola' is similar but with larger blooms borne in greater profusion. This species is best planted in a sheltered spot or in mild areas.

R. filipes 'Kiftsgate' produces large heads of many small, creamy-white flowers that are sweetly scented. The blooms are followed by ornamental hips in autumn. *R. f.* 'Brenda Colvin' is similar but with flowers that are blush-pink to start with before aging to white.

Rambler roses that grow to around 7.3 m (25 ft) include 'Bobbie James' which has very large heads of fragrant, creamy-white, semi-double flowers, 'Paul's Himalayan Musk', a handsome rose bearing many clusters of tiny, pale pink flowers, and 'Wedding Day' which produces huge heads of flowers that open creamy-yellow and quickly age to white.

Annual climbers

These one-year wonders offer the greatest versatility of all the climbing plants. Speed of growth is their obvious appeal, and annual climbers can quickly give an established look to a brand-new garden by filling gaps between newly planted, permanent climbers and wall shrubs. Grow them up supports in borders to introduce some height quickly, through other plants for an extra burst of flowers, and in containers to create a column of summer colour. On the other hand, if your garden is packed full of permanent plants, it's always possible to squeeze in a few annuals.

The fascination of growing beautiful, flourishing plants from little, wizened seeds is unending, and I never cease to be amazed at the amount of growth that can be produced in so short a time. From spring-sown seed comes a mass of stems that are usually covered in flowers within about three months of sowing. You don't need green fingers or a greenhouse either. Plants like nasturtiums are extremely easy to grow – just push the seed into the ground and away they go! Certain other plants need to be grown with a bit of love and attention, but there is something for every level of interest and experience. This group of plants encompasses both hardy annuals (HA) which tolerate frost and can therefore be sown outside in autumn or spring, and half-hardy annuals (HHA) which are completely frost-tender and are thus best raised under cover in gentle heat and planted out in late spring or early summer. All the plants listed here prefer a sunny site, and unless stated otherwise they all reach about 1.5–1.8 m (5–6 ft).

Cardiospermum halicacabum (balloon vine or love-in-a-puff) is most notable for its curious, inflated seed pods that cover the plant in mid- to late summer. This vigorous climber has attractive, dense, feathery foliage that is ideal for disguising the ugly lines of chain-link fencing or any other unsightly objects. Height 2.4–3 m (8–10 ft).

Cobaea scandens (cup-and-saucer plant) quickly produces long, rambling stems 4–4.8 m (13–16 ft) long, and in late summer it bears large, trumpet-shaped purple flowers with a 'ruff' at the base – the saucer to the cup. The form 'Alba' has attractive, greenish-white flowers. This plant can be perennial in very mild areas, but it performs best when treated as an annual and grown in a sunny spot. HHA.

Eccremocarpus scaber can be treated as an annual, though it is actually perennial. See page 113.

Gourds are grown for their striking and unusually shaped, ornamental fruits, which are borne in late summer. Mostly orange and yellow, they come in all sorts of weird and wonderful shapes – the aptly named variety 'Choose your Weapon' gives some idea of what to expect. The fruits make lovely indoor decorations, and they can be painted with a coat of clear varnish to intensify their glowing colours even further. Gourds belong to the same family as marrows, and they have similar preferences of full sun and rich soil in order to produce a good crop of fruits. However, the foliage is large and coarse, so it's best not to put gourds in very prominent positions. HHA.

Ipomoea includes some supremely beautiful and exotic plants, my favourite being *Ipomoea tricolor* 'Heavenly Blue' (morning glory) with huge, saucer-shaped blooms that are a deep and exquisite sky-blue with a white centre. The individual flowers last for only a day, but they are borne in such profusion as to ensure a near-continuous supply. White- and red-flowered forms are also available. The flowers of *I. quamoclit* (*Mina lobata*) are totally different, being tubular and borne on short stems. At first the flowers are crimson and then gradually age to yellow, so at any time a stem of flowers can be an attractive mixture of colours. *Ipomoea* like a sunny, sheltered spot and rich, well-drained soil. Height 2.4–3 m (8–10 ft). HHA.

Lathyrus species include that well-loved favourite, the sweet pea (*Lathyrus odoratus*). These charming, often highly scented flowers, in a rainbow mixture of colours, were highly fashionable in Edwardian times and they have remained popular with gardeners ever since. The flowers are ideal for cutting, particularly as regular deadheading is necessary to stimulate continued flower production. Sweet peas thrive in rich, deep, moisture-retentive soil. I find it really pays to prepare the soil in advance of planting by

digging a trench and filling it with retentive material such as well-rotted manure or kitchen waste which is then covered with several centimetres of soil. Such preparation is extremely valuable on free-draining soils.

Other annual species include *L. sativus* (Indian pea) which bears small stems of flowers that are an exquisite azure blue. Height 1–1.2 m (3–4 ft). *L. tingitanus* (Tangier scarlet pea) produces showy, purple-and-scarlet flowers that are ideal for cutting. As well as the species, there is a mixed variety available that includes mauve, pink and white forms. HA.

Maurandya barclayana is a handsome plant bearing large, funnel-shaped flowers in beautiful shades of soft rose-pink. It is a vigorous grower, producing long stems of up to 3 m (10 ft), which are clothed with pale green leaves. *M. scandens* is less vigorous and the flowers are smaller but just as pretty, in a range of charming colours including lilac, violet-blue and pure white. HHA.

Rhodochiton atrosanguineus (purple bell vine) is definitely one for lovers of the unusual. Its flowers are of such a dark shade of purple as to appear almost black, with a dark 'ruff' at the base and a long, tubular corolla. It can be perennial if it is overwintered in a frost-free place. HHA.

~

*The purple bell vine (*Rhodochiton*) has unusually shaped, deep maroon flowers that appear to be almost black. They show up best against a white background.*

Thunbergia alata (black-eyed Susan) is an old, easily grown favourite, bearing orange, yellow or white flowers with a striking black 'eye', on twining stems. HHA.

Tropaeolum majus (nasturtium) is the easiest annual of all to grow. Within just a few weeks of pushing the seeds into the soil, you will find long, rambling stems and masses of bright flowers in glowing shades of red, orange and yellow. An extra bonus is that both leaves and flowers are edible: add the leaves to a salad to give it a peppery, spicy flavour and scatter the flowers on top for a colourful decoration. The young seeds can be used as substitutes for capers.

T. perigrinum (canary creeper) is also quick and easy to grow, with small, fresh green, lobed leaves and bright yellow flowers prettily fringed at the edges. Height 2.4–3 m (8–10 ft). Both these plants will often self-seed, so new seedlings may pop up the next year without any further encouragement from you! HA.

Herbaceous climbers

Climbing plants that die back to the ground in autumn and regrow rapidly in spring have particular benefits for certain sites around the garden. There may be places where a permanent area of growth could be a problem, such as a wooden structure where access for maintenance is necessary, for example, or around an oil tank. Herbaceous climbers are ideal for growing through shrubs, because

they can rarely produce enough growth in one year to exert a stranglehold on their host. Most of these plants are quick-growing into the bargain, so they are good for giving an established air to a new garden. Pruning in all cases is limited to simply cutting back dead growth to ground level during the winter. Practical considerations aside, this group includes some plants of especial charm and beauty that I would be hard put to do without in my garden. In addition to the plants listed below *Clematis viticella* and cultivars can be treated almost as herbaceous plants.

Aconitum hemsleyanum (climbing aconite) bears stems of hooded, mauve flowers on thin, scrambling stems in late summer and autumn. Rather than being showy in its own right, this plant is best partnered with a shrub, preferably one with gold or silver foliage to make the mauve flowers stand out well. As in the case of all aconites, every part of the plant is poisonous. It thrives in part- or full shade. Height 1.2–1.8 m (4–6 ft).

Dicentra macrocapnos and *D. scandens* are unusual and attractive relatives of the popular bleeding heart (*Dicentra spectabilis*). Yellow, locket-like flowers are borne in dangling bunches of eight to twelve blooms from late summer to early autumn, against delicate, fern-like leaves. The plant scrambles up by means of tendrils, so it is best grown through a shrub, or up wire mesh or pea sticks. It can be raised fairly easily from spring-sown seed and prefers partial shade. Height approx. 1.8 m (6 ft).

Eccremocarpus scaber (Chilean glory flower) is a fast-growing plant, scrambling up by means of tendrils. It keeps its foliage in warmer areas but tends to die back to the ground if hard frosts occur. From mid-summer it bears stems of exotic, tubular, brightly coloured flowers, usually orange but sometimes red and yellow too. It grows readily from spring-sown seed and tends to flower well in its first year. This plant needs full sun in order to perform well. Height 1.8 m (6 ft).

Humulus lupulus 'Aureus' (golden hop) is an invaluable plant, in part because there are so few climbers with golden foliage. In spring the stems twine up wires or canes with amazing speed and they are soon covered with large, lobed, yellow-green leaves. By late summer the foliage is strongly suffused with green. Female plants – which unfortunately are less common in cultivation than the males – bear large, decorative seed heads that give off a rich, beery aroma when crushed. The dried seed heads can be made into a fragrant hop pillow – a traditional remedy for sleeplessness. It does well in sun or part shade. Height 3 m (10 ft).

Lathyrus (perennial pea) includes some immensely beautiful species that can be used in a wealth of places around the garden. Although they lack the fragrance of their popular annual cousins, the beauty and profusion of their flowers more than compensates for it. Climbing by means of tendrils, they can be grown up wire mesh or pea sticks and through other plants, or even left unsupported to tumble down a sunny bank. *Lathyrus latifolius* is an old cottage-garden favourite with bright pink flowers that have the potential to clash alarmingly with many other garden plants, though fortunately the paler 'Pink Pearl' is much easier to place. The lovely 'White Pearl' bears pearly-white flowers. *L. rotundifolius* (Persian everlasting pea) has supremely attractive blooms that are light pink on the outside and a deep pinky-red shade in the centre. Masses of fresh green leaves make a good backdrop to the flowers. Perennial peas do best in sun and well-drained soil. Height 1.8–2.4 m (6–8 ft). Keen gardeners may be interested in growing *Lathyrus nervosus* (Lord Anson's blue pea) with flowers that are an exquisite shade of deep, clear blue. Height 1.2 m (4 ft).

Tropaeolum species belong to the same family as the annual garden nasturtiums, though the perennial forms are more particular about their requirements than the grow-anywhere annuals. However, their masses of superbly colourful flowers make them well worth the effort. *Tropaeolum speciosum* (Scotch flame flower) bears lots of little scarlet flowers in early summer that mass together to create an eye-catching blaze of colour. Its many thin stems are best supported by another plant, such as a dark-foliaged conifer or even a hedge. It thrives in cool, moist conditions and quickly became popular last century in lowland Scotland's gardens; this resulted in its common name, although it is a native of Chile. In warmer areas it is best planted in a shady spot. Height 1.8–2.4 m (6–8 ft).

The golden hop (Humulus lupulus 'Aureus') is one of the best herbaceous climbers. The whole plant dies back to the ground in winter but it regrows rapidly in spring.

~

T. *tuberosum*, on the other hand, relishes a warm, sunny site and well-drained soil. In late summer it bears many tubular, orange-scarlet flowers on short stems. The form 'Ken Aslet' is especially free-flowering. Although hardy in a sheltered spot, in colder areas it is wise to lift a few of the tuberous roots for overwintering in a frost-free place. Treat like dahlia tubers, keeping them in just-moist compost to avoid shrivelling and checking regularly for rot. Height 1.8 m (6 ft).

Frost-tender climbers

Those climbers that are on the borderline of hardiness include some superbly beautiful exotic plants. Where the weather is harsh they can be grown under cover in a conservatory, but in mild areas they may remain outside all year if they are given the protection of a sunny, sheltered wall. It is worth bearing in mind that in cities the temperature tends to be artificially higher by several degrees than in the countryside.

Compact-growing plants could also be kept in pots on the patio for the summer and moved into a frost-free environment during winter. Either way these plants can be used to give an extra-special lift to the summer garden or conservatory.

However, this chapter is not intended to be a comprehensive list of plants for the conservatory, as it covers only those which are suitable for a protected environment that is heated just enough to be frost-free in winter. A conservatory heated to a minimum of about 10°C (50°F) in winter is suitable for a much wider range of tender plants.

Billardiera longiflora is attractive in both flowers and fruit. In summer it bears pretty little bell-shaped blooms of lime-green, an unusual flower colour, and these are followed by oblong, deep blue fruits that can be up to 2.5 cm (1 in) long. In mild areas it can be planted outside to scramble over a bush, and inside it can be trained on wires up a wall. The slender, twining stems grow up to 1.8 m (6 ft) high. Evergreen.

Clianthus puniceus (parrot's bill or lobster's claw) is so named for its eye-catching and unusual flowers, which are borne in dangling racemes in early summer. The blooms of the species are brilliant red, *C. p.* 'Roseus' (also called 'Flamingo') is deep pink and *C. p.* 'Albus' (also known as 'White Heron') is pure white flushed with green. The large, pinnate leaves are semi-evergreen. The stems of this vigorous shrub need tying in to trellis or wires. Height 2.4 m (8 ft). Deciduous.

~

Clianthus puniceus *is an exotic plant, one of a number that tolerate little or no frost.*

Dregea sinensis (formerly *Wattakaka*) is a climber that bears deliciously scented flowers in summer; these are white with a central mass of red spots. The twining stems grow to around 3 m (10 ft) high. Deciduous.

Gelsemium sempervirens (yellow jessamine) is a jasmine-like plant with long, twining stems clad with glossy, green leaves. The flowers are trumpet-shaped and bright yellow, shaded rich orange in the throat and up to 2.5 cm (1 in) long. They are borne in

late spring or early summer and are sweetly scented too. Height 3 m (10 ft). Evergreen.

Jasmines that are frost-tender include *Jasminum azoricum*, a twining plant which bears clusters of white, sweetly scented flowers in late summer and often into winter. *J. mesnyi* (primrose jasmine) is a handsome evergreen with long, winding shoots that need tying in to their support. During spring it bears large, bright yellow flowers that are delicately scented and which are shown off beautifully by the dark green foliage. Height 1.8 m (6 ft).

J. *polyanthum* is often sold as a small pot plant, but, given a large pot or a place in the border soil of a conservatory, it will develop into a sizeable, handsome plant up to 4.5 m (15 ft) high. White, pink-flushed flowers are borne in large clusters from late spring through summer, and they have a strong and delicious scent. There are other, less common jasmines that need conservatory protection such as *J. angulare*.

Lapageria rosea (Chilean bellflower) has glorious flowers that make almost any gardener want to grow it, but this plant does have exacting requirements. It needs a cool, moist, lime-free soil and full or part-shade in order to thrive and produce it stunning, deep rose-red trumpets of flowers that have thick, waxy-textured petals. The blooms of *L. r.* 'Nash Court' are clear pink in colour. The tough, twining stems are clothed with leathery, dark green leaves. Height up to 3 m (10 ft). Evergreen.

Mandevilla laxa (Chilean jasmine) bears white, sweetly scented flowers in summer, which are up to 5 cm (2 in) across and rather like those of a periwinkle in appearance. It has twining, slender stems and attractive heart-shaped leaves. This species is well worth growing for the sweet scent of its blooms, whereas *M.* x *amoena* 'Alice du Pont' has exceptionally beautiful flowers but unfortunately no fragrance. The blooms are large, trumpet-shaped and a lovely shade of deep glowing pink. Height up to 3.6 m (12 ft). Deciduous.

Passiflora species (passion flowers) for mild areas or conservatories include several with spectacular and ornate blooms that nestle on single stalks among handsome, lobed leaves. If the summer weather has been favourable, fruits are often produced, and the pulp that surrounds their many seeds is edible. They can be cut hard back in late winter if necessary.

P. x 'Allardii' has pink-and-white flowers with a central corona of white and deep blue. *P. antioquiensis* has a mixture of lobed and unlobed leaves, and it bears striking, rich rose-red flowers with a violet-blue corona. The flowers of *P. racemosa* (red passion flower) are scarlet with purple, white-tipped outer filaments. Height approx. 3–4 m (10–13 ft).

Sollya heterophylla (bluebell creeper) is a pretty, twining climber that bears clusters of delicate and beautiful sky-blue flowers in summer and autumn. It prefers a lime-free soil. Height 1.8 m (6 ft).

Tecoma capensis (Cape honeysuckle) is a vigorous plant bearing bright scarlet, trumpet-shaped flowers in clusters on the ends of its stems in late summer. The self-clinging or twining stems are clothed with bold, attractive, pinnate leaves. Carry out any necessary pruning in late winter by shortening side shoots by about half. Height up to 4 m (13 ft). Deciduous.

Tweedia caerulea (also known as *Oxypetalum caeruleum*) is a small, neat, twining plant with clusters of flowers that are a beautiful and almost unreal shade of powder-blue and heart-shaped, grey-green leaves. It can be grown easily from seed sown in spring. Height 1–1.2 m (3–4 ft). Deciduous.

Edible climbers

Plants that are edible as well as ornamental combine the best of all possible worlds and there are few experiences in gardening to beat the joy of growing, harvesting and then eating a crop. These plants make it possible for small-space gardeners to produce a real feast even when there is no room at all for a special kitchen garden.

Many edible climbers look good too, so they are perfectly at home rubbing shoulders with plants that are purely ornamental. Forget the old discipline of segregating fruit and veg. from the ornamental garden, and instead mingle runner beans with sweet peas, train loganberries over an archway and cover a wall with a mass of fruit-tree blossom. Just

bear in mind that, for the best results, fruiting plants need a good soil and full sun, though most will crop reasonably in partial shade.

Fruit

Berry fruits such as blackberries and loganberries bear heavy crops of luscious fruit in summer and early autumn. For the rest of the year, though, they aren't very attractive, so these plants tend to be best sited away from the most prominent parts of the garden. They can be trained against a fence or wall, but because they are fairly vigorous they do need a fair amount of room to spread – preferably allow 1.8–3 m (6–10 ft) between plants. They can also be grown on a post-and-wire framework, made by erecting stout fence posts 1.8 m (6 ft) high with strong, galvanized wires running between them. The first wire should be 60 cm (24 in) from the ground with the remaining ones 30–45 cm (12–18 in) apart.

The fruit produced by cultivated blackberries bears little relation to that of the wild 'brambles'. Varieties such as 'Bedford Giant' and 'Himalaya' produce large, well-flavoured berries that freeze well. In addition to blackberries and loganberries, there are some interesting hybrid berries such as the tayberry and boysenberry.

Most berry fruits are well endowed with vicious thorns, so it's advisable to site them well away from paths or gateways where they can snag unwary passers-by. However, in a similar vein, they could be useful for keeping unwanted visitors at bay! Fortunately there are several attractive, thorn-free varieties, such as blackberry 'Oregon Thornless' and 'Merton Thornless', and loganberry 'LY654'.

Annual pruning encourages fruit production and keeps the plant within bounds. First of all, cut the whole plant to 23 cm (9 in) from the ground immediately after planting, which encourages the formation of strong, new shoots. Then every year, after the fruit has been harvested, cut out all the old branches that have borne fruit and tie in the new ones, spreading them out so that they all get plenty of light and air. Pruning is made much easier if the new shoots are kept separate from the old ones – say, by training the old one to the right and keeping the new growths to the left.

Kiwi fruit or Chinese gooseberry (*Actinidia chinensis*) really needs a sunny, sheltered spot

~

Fruit trees fit well into a small garden if they are grown against a sunny wall. This pear tree has been trained in horizontal tiers, though it's also possible to grow trees in fan or cordon shapes.

in a reasonably mild area in order to produce its oval, olive-green, hairy fruits. Until recently it was necessary to have two plants, a male and a female, in order that pollination could occur and fruit be produced. However, the introduction of self-fertile varieties such as 'Issai' means that fruit can be produced from just one plant. The kiwi fruit is a vigorous, twining climber with large, heart-shaped leaves, and it can grow up to 5.1 m (17 ft).

Trees

Tree fruits such as apples, pears and plums that are specially trained in fan, espalier and cordon shapes can be grown flat against walls and fences, and cordons can even be trained over an arch. Fan-trained trees, as their name suggests, have branches radiating outwards in a fan shape. The branches of espalier trees are trained horizontally, normally in two tiers. Cordons, on the other hand, consist of one main stem that is trained at an angle of 45 degrees, which makes it possible to plant several cordons in a row at a spacing of 75–90 cm (2½–3 ft) between plants. Fans and espaliers are best bought as two-to-three-year-old trees that have been ready-trained, unless you fancy training your own, while for cordons it's generally best to start with one-year-old maiden trees.

Apples and pears can be grown in all three the shapes described above, while plums, cherries, apricots, nectarines and peaches are available only as fan-trained trees. Some types, particularly apples and pears, need to be pollinated in order to produce fruit, in which case it's necessary to grow two different varieties together so that their flowers can be fertilized. They must be of the same type – for example, a pear cannot pollinate an apple – and flower at the same time so that pollen can be exchanged. If in any doubt, check at the nursery before buying your trees. If you want a fan or espalier, it is possible to obtain a family tree – that is, a tree that has been specially grafted so that it is made up of two or three different varieties – though you may have to buy this from a specialist nursery.

Growing a fruit tree against a wall or fence has several advantages. The sheltered environment helps protect the blossom from frost and aids ripening of the fruit. If late frosts threaten to damage the blossom, it is comparatively easy to protect the tree with a roll of polythene or horticultural fleece. However, shortage of water can be a problem, so it's a good idea to prepare the ground very thoroughly before planting, adding plenty of organic matter, and to water when necessary during dry spells. Remember to add fertilizer regularly, too.

When planting, take care to plant the tree at the same depth as it was growing previously, so that the lumpy graft union on the stem is above the soil. Plant cordons with this graft union uppermost, otherwise it can be put under stress when the tree leans.

To hold the tree firm against the wall, fix strong, galvanized wires about 45–60 cm (18–24 in) apart. Tie the branches to the wires with twine, soft string, or even pieces of old nylon tights, but don't use wire or nylon string as it can easily cut into the bark.

How to prune trained fruit trees

Cordon apples and pears should be pruned in winter by cutting back all side shoots to about 7.5 cm (3 in) long. On older trees thin out the fruiting spurs if there are so many that they become congested. In summer prune any new side shoots as above, and shorten to 2.5 cm (1 in) any shoots coming from the side shoots pruned earlier.

Fan and espalier-trained apples and pears should have their side shoots pruned in the same way.

Prune plums, sweet cherries and apricots in spring by thinning out dense or outward-pointing shoots that rise from the main framework of branches. In summer pinch out shoot tips once five or six leaves have developed, and after fruiting cut these same shoots back by half.

Peaches, nectarines and acid cherries should have their side shoots thinned in spring to leave one every 10 cm (4 in) or so. Pinch out the tips of last year's side shoots once four to six leaves have developed. This will encourage more side shoots to grow from the base, and, after harvest, last year's side shoots should be pruned out to leave the new ones for next year.

Grapevines

Grapevines are quick-growing plants with handsome leaves that are lovely to grow over the top of an arbour or pergola to create a dappled shade, reminiscent of Continental cafes. Their bunches of fruit are decorative as well as mouth-wateringly tempting, though in a cool climate grapes need a favoured site to produce a reasonable crop. Grow them in a warm, sheltered spot away from frost pockets, in a reasonably fertile soil that is well drained. It's best to avoid ground that is too rich as foliage would be produced at the expense of fruit. They prefer a soil pH of 6.0–7.5. It's important to water regularly until the fruit starts to ripen. Generally grapes for wine-making are more successful outside in cool areas, while dessert varieties are better grown under glass. A few varieties such as 'Madeleine Angevine', 'Madeleine Sylvaner' and 'Black Hamburgh' are suitable for both purposes. A framework of wires is best for training grapes, with the top wire about 1.2 m (4 ft) from the ground.

How to prune grapevines

1. After planting cut back the main stem to three buds and train the resulting three shoots straight up a cane.

2. In autumn or winter carefully bend two shoots horizontally either side and cut the third shoot to three buds, training the subsequent shoots vertically as before.

3. Next year the two horizontal shoots will produce a number of side shoots that will grow upwards and bear fruit. Pinch out these side shoots when they reach the top wire and pinch out any smaller lateral shoots.

4. In autumn or winter the two main horizontal shoots should be cut out completely, and the process starts again from step 2.

Vegetables

Runner beans are ideal for some swift cover as well as a quick crop, with colourful flowers and masses of tasty beans. Choose from traditional red-flowered varieties such as 'Streamline' or 'Scarlet Emperor', white ones like 'Desirée', or the old-fashioned 'Painted Lady' with pretty bi-coloured flowers. Climbing french beans are similar, though a little more tolerant of difficult conditions than runner beans.

Beans like a deep, moisture-retentive soil, and for the best results it is well worth preparing a trench in advance of planting. Simply dig a hole about 45 cm (18 in) deep and fill it with any organic matter that holds water well, such as rotted manure, compost, shredded newspaper, kitchen waste and even the vacuum-cleaner bag contents. Cover the trench with a layer of soil and leave it to settle for a while before planting.

The lablab or hyacinth bean, is related to the runner bean, *Lablab purpureus* but it is even more ornamental, with large, purple-green leaves, and mauve flowers that are followed by dark purple, velvety beans.

Marrows and squashes that have a trailing habit can be trained up low supports, and they are a real feast for the eye in summer with their large, attractive fruits. Those of the marrow are plain green or striped, but it is the squashes that are really ornamental, particularly the 'patty pan' or custard varieties that are cream or yellow in colour with attractively scalloped edges. As with runner beans, they flourish in a good, deep, moisture-retentive soil.

Suppliers

Products

Growing bag frames

Loral Products Ltd
Loral House
Badingham
Suffolk   IP13 8LG
Tel/Fax: 01728 638677

Trompe l'oeil *features*

Frolics of Winchester
83 Canon Street
Winchester
Hampshire SO23 9JQ
Tel: 01962 856384
Fax: 01962 844896

The Honeysuckle Group
Lysander Road
Bowerhill
Melksham
Wiltshire SN12 6UR
Tel: 01225 709033
Fax: 01225 790060

Willow arches and tripods

The English Basket & Hurdle Centre
Curload
Stoke St Gregory
Taunton
Somerset TA3 6JD
Tel: 01823 698418
Fax: 01823 698859

Touch Designs
PO Box 60
Andover
Hampshire SP11 6SS
Tel: 01264 738060

Wooden pergolas, arches and trellis

Forest Fencing Ltd
Stanford Court
Stanford Bridge
Worcester WR6 6SR
Tel: 01886 812451
Fax: 01886 812343

Hill Hout Ltd
Harfreys Road
Harfreys Industrial Estate
Great Yarmouth
Norfolk NR31 0LS
Tel: 01493 440017
Fax: 01493 440019

Larch-Lap Ltd
PO Box 17
Lichfield Street
Stourport-on-Severn
Worcestershire DY13 9ES
Tel: 01299 823232
Fax: 01299 871534

Steel, wire and wrought-iron supports

Agriframes Ltd
Charlwoods Road
East Grinstead

West Sussex RH19 2HG
Tel: 01342 328644
Fax: 01342 327233

Rayments Wirework
The Forge, Durlock
Minster
Thanet
Kent CT12 4HE
Tel: 01843 821628

Samsons
Edwin Avenue
Hoo Farm Industrial Estate
Worcester Road
Kidderminster
Worcestershire DY11 7RA
Tel: 01562 825252
Fax: 01562 820380

Plants

Clematis

Great Dixter Nurseries
Northiam
Rye
East Sussex TN31 6PH
Tel: 01797 253107
Fax: 01797 252879

The Valley Clematis Nursery
Willingham Road
Hainton
Lincoln LN3 6LN
Tel: 01507 313398
Fax: 01507 313705

Climbers, wall shrubs and fruiting plants

Burncoose Nurseries
Gwennap
Redruth
Cornwall TR16 6BJ
Tel: 01209 861112
Fax: 01209 860011

Notcutts Nurseries Ltd
Woodbridge
Suffolk IP12 4AF
Tel: 01394 383344
Fax: 01394 385460

Roses

David Austin Roses
Bowling Green Lane
Albrighton
Wolverhampton WV7 3HB
Tel: 01902 373931
Fax: 01902 372142

Mattocks Roses
Nuneham Courtenay
Oxford X44 9PY
Tel: 01865 343265

Seeds

Chiltern Seeds
Bortree Stile
Ulverston
Cumbria LA12 7PB
Tel: 01229 581137
Fax: 01229 584549

Unwins Seeds Ltd
Histon
Cambridge
CB4 4ZZ
Tel: 01945 588522

Tender climbers

Read's Nursery
Hales Hall
Loddon
Norfolk NR4 6QW
Tel: 01508 548395
Fax: 01508 548040

Index

Page references in bold indicate main entry in the plant directory, those in italics indicate illustrations.